First World War
and Army of Occupation
War Diary
France, Belgium and Germany

46 DIVISION
139 Infantry Brigade,
Brigade Machine Gun Company
16 February 1916 - 28 February 1918

WO95/2695/3

The Naval & Military Press Ltd
www.nmarchive.com
Published in association with The National Archives

Published by

The Naval & Military Press Ltd

Unit 10 Ridgewood Industrial Park,

Uckfield, East Sussex,

TN22 5QE England

Tel: +44 (0) 1825 749494

www.naval-military-press.com

www.nmarchive.com

This diary has been reprinted in facsimile from the original. Any imperfections are inevitably reproduced and the quality may fall short of modern type and cartographic standards.

© **Crown Copyright**
Images reproduced by permission of The National Archives, London, England, 2015.

Contents

Document type	Place/Title	Date From	Date To
Heading	WO95/2695 (3)		
Heading	46th Division 139th Infy Bde 139th Machine Gun Coy. Feb 1916-Feb 1918		
War Diary	Bernaville	16/02/1916	19/02/1916
War Diary	Barlette	20/02/1916	29/02/1916
War Diary	Beauval	06/03/1916	06/03/1916
War Diary	Berlencourt	08/03/1916	08/03/1916
War Diary	Mt. St Eloy	09/03/1916	31/03/1916
Diagram etc	Gun Positions Taken Over from the French Army by 139th Bde M.G. Coy		
War Diary	Mont. St. Eloy	01/04/1916	20/04/1916
War Diary	Bethencourt	23/04/1916	29/04/1916
War Diary	Averdoigmt	30/04/1916	30/04/1916
War Diary	Averdoingt	02/05/1916	05/05/1916
War Diary	Canettemont	06/05/1916	06/05/1916
War Diary	Gaudiempre	06/05/1916	16/05/1916
War Diary	Fonquevillers	18/05/1916	31/05/1916
Miscellaneous	Machine Gun Company 139th Brigade	06/07/1916	06/07/1916
War Diary	Fonquevillers	01/06/1916	03/06/1916
War Diary	Humbercamp	04/06/1916	06/06/1916
War Diary	Brevillers	07/06/1916	17/06/1916
War Diary	Pommier	18/06/1916	29/06/1916
War Diary		28/06/1916	30/06/1916
Miscellaneous	Machine Gun Company 139th Brigade	02/08/1916	02/08/1916
War Diary	Fonquevillers	01/07/1916	02/07/1916
War Diary	Warlincourt	03/07/1916	03/07/1916
War Diary	Saulty	04/07/1916	10/07/1916
War Diary	Bellacourt	11/07/1916	31/07/1916
War Diary		29/07/1916	31/07/1916
Operation(al) Order(s)	Operation Orders by Capt. F.B. Robinson Commanding 139th Brigade Machine Gun Company		
Diagram etc			
Diagram etc	Fonquevillers		
Diagram etc	Scale 1:5,000 1st Objective 2nd 56th Division Figures and Denotes Time Artillery Fire Lifts Off Trench		
Miscellaneous	139th Machine Gun Company	02/09/1916	02/09/1916
War Diary	Bellacourt	03/08/1916	28/08/1916
War Diary		01/08/1916	01/08/1916
War Diary	Bellacourt	14/09/1916	25/09/1916
War Diary	Grosville	26/09/1916	30/10/1916
War Diary	Sus-St-Leger	01/11/1916	01/11/1916
War Diary	Caneleux	03/11/1916	03/11/1916
War Diary	Hiermont	06/11/1916	06/11/1916
War Diary	Neuville D'onex	11/11/1916	11/11/1916
War Diary	Hiermont	22/11/1916	22/11/1916
War Diary	St Acheul	23/11/1916	23/11/1916
War Diary	Occoches	25/11/1916	25/11/1916
War Diary	Warluzel	29/11/1916	30/11/1916
War Diary	Fonquevillers	05/12/1916	30/01/1917
War Diary	Fonquevillers	01/01/1917	17/03/1917

War Diary	Souastre	18/03/1917	20/03/1917
War Diary	Bayencourt	21/03/1917	23/03/1917
War Diary	Contay	24/03/1917	24/03/1917
War Diary	Villers Bocage	25/03/1917	25/03/1917
War Diary		24/03/1917	24/03/1917
War Diary	St. Fuscien	26/03/1917	27/03/1917
War Diary	Ligny-Lez-Aire	28/03/1917	09/04/1917
War Diary	Chocques	13/04/1917	13/04/1917
War Diary	Noeux-Les-Mines	14/04/1917	16/04/1917
War Diary	Angres	19/04/1917	20/04/1917
War Diary	Lievin	21/04/1917	30/04/1917
War Diary	Bully Grenay	01/05/1917	02/05/1917
War Diary	St. Pierre	06/05/1917	19/05/1917
War Diary	Bully Grenay	19/05/1917	23/05/1917
War Diary	Lievin	25/05/1917	12/06/1917
War Diary	St. Pierre	15/06/1917	03/07/1917
War Diary	Frevillers	04/07/1917	24/07/1917
War Diary	Vermelles	25/07/1917	16/08/1917
War Diary	Fouquieres	18/08/1917	20/08/1917
War Diary	Drouvin	22/08/1917	25/08/1917
War Diary	Annequin	27/08/1917	30/08/1917
War Diary	Cambrin Sector. Annequin	01/09/1917	17/09/1917
War Diary	Sailly Labourse	19/09/1917	23/09/1917
War Diary	Mazingarbe 14.Bis. Sector	24/09/1917	30/09/1917
War Diary		29/09/1917	29/09/1917
War Diary	Mazingarbe. 14. Bis. Sector.	29/09/1917	29/09/1917
Miscellaneous	139th Machine Gun Company	06/09/1917	06/09/1917
Miscellaneous	139th Machine Gun Company	24/09/1917	24/09/1917
Miscellaneous	139th Machine Gun Company Disposition of Guns Cambrin Sector.	26/08/1917	26/08/1917
War Diary	Mazingarbe	01/10/1917	31/10/1917
War Diary		29/10/1917	29/10/1917
War Diary	Mazingarbe	01/11/1917	16/11/1917
War Diary	Vermelles	17/11/1917	31/12/1917
War Diary	Vermelles H2 Brewers	01/01/1918	12/01/1918
War Diary	Vermelles	13/01/1918	23/01/1918
War Diary	Cense La Vallee	24/01/1918	07/02/1918
War Diary	Hurion Ville	08/02/1918	08/02/1918
War Diary	Petigny	09/02/1918	28/02/1918

WO97/2695(3)

WO97/2695(3)

46TH DIVISION
139TH INFY BDE

139TH MACHINE GUN COY.

FEB 1916-FEB 1918

WAR DIARY or INTELLIGENCE SUMMARY

Army Form C. 2118

(Erase heading not required.)

Place	Date	Hour	Summary of Events and Information	Remarks and references to Appendices
BERNAVILLE	1916 Feb. 16	3 p.m.	BDE. M.G. COY. formed from personnel of 5th, 6th, 7th & 8th SHERWOOD FORESTERS M.G. Sections. Officers: CAPT. F.B. ROBINSON O.C. — 6th SHERWOOD FORESTERS. LIEUT. M.C. WOLLASTON — 5th " " " T.H.F. ADAMS acting adjt — 8th " " " G.F. GARDNER — 6th " " 2nd " E.B. WOODFORDE — 5th " " " T. GRIMSHAW — 6th " " " W.H. REZIN — 8th " " " E.J. PEACH — 7th " " " J.E. KEMSHALL — 7th " "	
"	19-16	10.15 a.m.	Moved to new billets at BARLETTE (3 miles) Map Ref. LENS 11 arrived BARLETTE 12. NOON.	
BARLETTE	20-16	10.0 a.m.	Inspection by Brigadier General Commanding. Several field movement carried out at inspection.	
"	21-16 to 28-16		Heavy snow & frost.	
"	29-16	9-30 a.m.	Moved to new billets at BEAUVAL (11 miles) Ref. Map. LENS 11. Arrived BEAUVAL 2 p.m. Progress interrupted by owing to heavy traffic on roads.	

WAR DIARY or INTELLIGENCE SUMMARY

Army Form C. 2118.

139th Bde. M.G. Coy

Place	Date	Hour	Summary of Events and Information	Remarks and references to Appendices
Beauval	6-3-16	8.30 A.M	Moved to new billets at Berlencourt (14 miles). Ref. Map. Lens II. Arrived Berlencourt 4 P.M.	
Berlencourt	8-3-16	9.0 A.M	Moved to new billets at Mont St Eloy (13 miles) Ref. Map. Lens II arrived Mt St Eloy 4 P.M.	
Mt St Eloy	9-3-16		Nos 3 & 4 Sections took over Gun Positions from 114th & 269th Regts. French Army (See Attached Map)	
"	10-3-16		No 2 Section took over Gun Positions from 125th Regt French Army (See Attached Map)	
"	13-3-16		Casualties 1 man wounded.	
"	15-3-16		Casualties 4 men accidentally wounded. 1 man has since died of wounds	
"	15-3-16 to 31-3-16		3 Sections in the trenches 1 in support at Mt St Eloy. Reliefs carried out every 12 days	

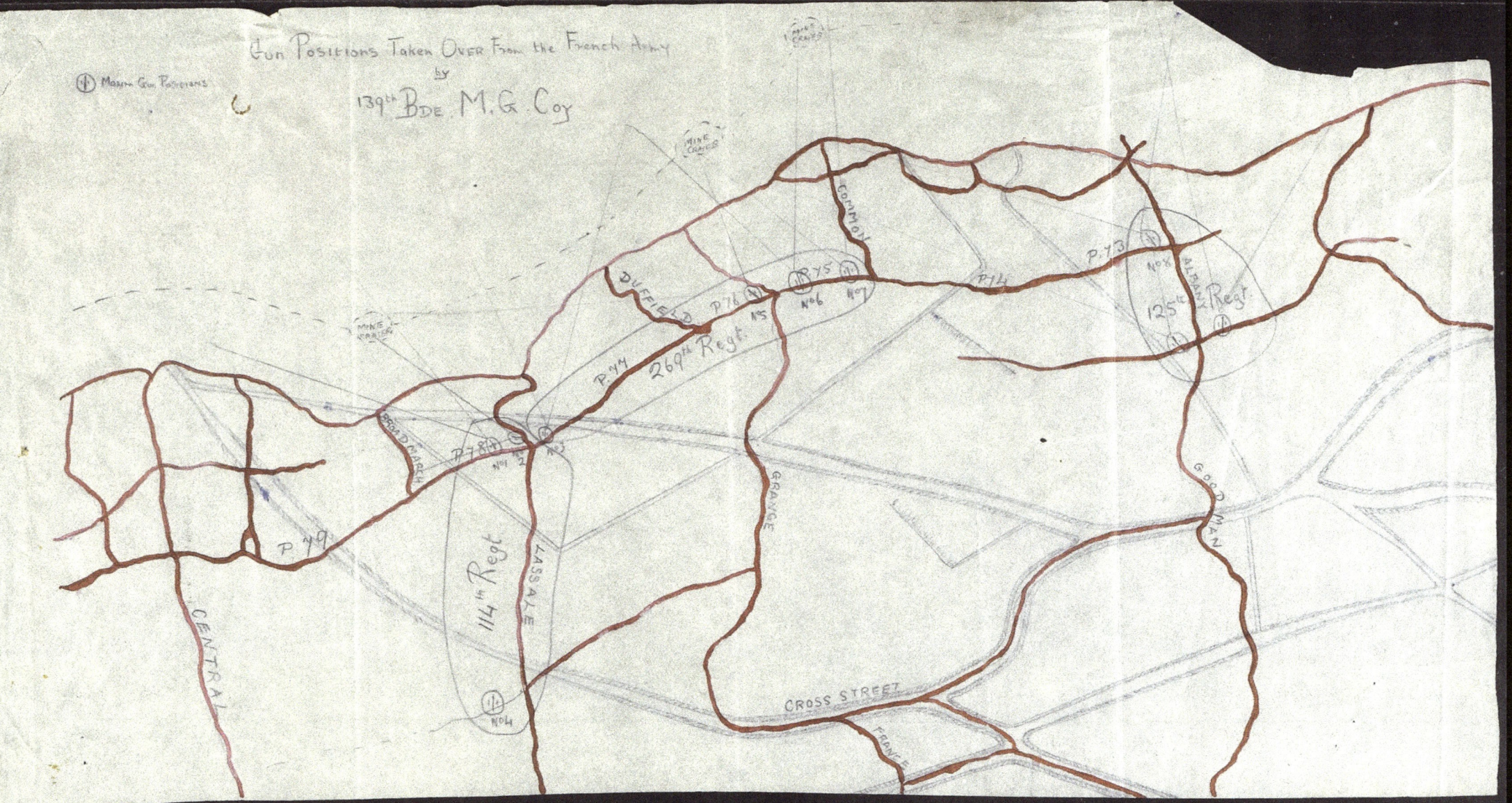

WAR DIARY
or
INTELLIGENCE SUMMARY
(Erase heading not required.)

Army Form C. 2118.

139th Brigade M.G. Coy.

Place	Date	Hour	Summary of Events and Information	Remarks and references to Appendices
Mont St Eloy	1/4/16 to 19/4/16		Occupied trenches with 138th Brigade on left & 137th Brigade on right. 3 Sections in the trenches and one in rest billets at MONT ST ELOY. Relief carried out every 4 day. Indirect fire employed nightly.	2879
	20/4/16		Cleaned up trenches preparatory to being relieved.	2879
	Night of 20/21st		Relieved by 7th Brigade Machine Gun Company. Relief completed by 1 p.m.	2879
			Proceeded by Motor Lorries to rest billets at BETHENCOURT. Arrived in billets 6 a.m.	
BETHENCOURT	23/4/16		Easter Day - Church Parade.	2879
BETHENCOURT	24/4/16 to 26/4/16		Usual training carried out for 4 hours daily.	
"	27/4/16	11 a.m.	Inspection by Brig. General Commanding 139th Brigade.	
	29/4/16	9 a.m.	Took over billets from the 138th Brigade M.G. Coy. at AVERDOINGT.	2879
AVERDOINGT	30/4/16	10 a.m.	Church Parade.	

H. Hollerton Lt
O.C. 139th Bde. M.G. Coy.

WAR DIARY or INTELLIGENCE SUMMARY

(Erase heading not required.)

139th Brigade Machine Gun Company

Vol 4

Army Form C. 2118

Place	Date 1916	Hour	Summary of Events and Information	Remarks and references to Appendices
AVERDOIGNT	May 2nd May 3rd	11 A.M.	Operations Practice in Smoke Attack in field near TINQUES.	Ref. Map.
AVERDOIGNT	May 5		Marched to new billeting area at CANETTEMONT. Marched under order of the O.C. 8th Batt. S. Forresters.	LEN 11
CANETTEMONT	May 6th		" " " " " GAUDIEMPRE Marched as a Brigade.	28pa
GAUDIEMPRE	May 6th to May 11		Usual training and instruction carried out. 4 hours daily.	28pa
GAUDIEMPRE	May 12th to May 16th		Company working for the 137th Brigade burying cables behind trenches at FONQUEVILLERS	28pa
FONQUEVILLERS	May 18		Night of 18th/19th Relieved the 137th Brigade in the Trenches at FONQUEVILLERS. 5 Guns in the front line - 9 Guns in emplacements in Support 2 Guns in Reserve in Village. Sketch Map attached.	28pa
FONQUEVILLERS	May 19		2nd Lieut W.R. CLAYTON M.G. Corps taken on Strength of Company. 19/5/16.	28pa
FONQUEVILLERS	May 19 to May 31.		Work carried out in improving old and constructing new emplacements. Very quiet. No Casualties.	28pa

O.C. 139 Bde M.G.C.

Machine Gun Company 139th Brigade

To

    D.A.G.

        3rd Echelon.

           Herewith War Diary of this Company from the 1st June to 30th June 1916.

                          for O.C. Machine Gun Company
                                 139th Brigade.

139th BRIGADE MACHINE GUN COMPANY.

No ....
Date ....

WAR DIARY or INTELLIGENCE SUMMARY

Army Form C. 2118.

(Erase heading not required.)

139th Brigade Machine Gun Company

Vol 5

Place	Date	Hour	Summary of Events and Information	Remarks and references to Appendices
FONQUEVILLERS	1916. June 1st & June 2nd		In Trenches – Work carried out in constructing new & improving old emplacements very quiet – no casualties	287a
	June 3rd		Company was relieved by the 138th Bde Machine Gun Company. Relief carried out after dark, completed by 1 a.m. – no casualties.	287a
HUMBERCAMP	June 4th & June 5th		In Rest billets – Men in huts – Company working on new railway.	287a
do.	June 6th		Company working on new railway 9 a.m. to 4 p.m. 7 p.m Company paraded and marched to SOUASTRE where busses were to convey men to new billets at BREVILLERS. Busses were not available and Company moved by route march – arrived in billets 6 a.m. 12 miles.	287a
BREVILLERS	June 7th		No parades. Men cleaning up in billets.	287a
do.	June 8th to 10th		Usual training carried out 5½ hours daily. Range practices daily.	287a
do.	June 11th		No Parades. Sunday.	287a
do.	June 12th & 13th		Range practices and usual training carried out 5½ hours daily.	287a
do.	June 14th to 17th		Practice in Scheme of Attack carried out on Brigade training ground near SUS-ST-LEGER	287a
do.	June 18th		Moved by route march to FONQUEVILLERS to take over 4 guns from the 138th Bde. M.G. Coy Halted in BIENVILLERS for dinners 3 hours – Relief to be carried out in daylight. The	

H. Wollaston Lt.

WAR DIARY or INTELLIGENCE SUMMARY

Army Form C. 2118.

(Erase heading not required.)

139th Brigade Machine Gun Company

Place	Date	Hour	Summary of Events and Information	Remarks and references to Appendices
	June 18th		Section taking the 4 guns in were bussed to BIENVILLERS and carried the guns from there to FONQUEVILLERS. On reaching trenches relief cancelled, company moved back back to billets at POMMIER.	2170.
POMMIER	June 19th		Company working under R.E. Officer at FONQUEVILLERS.	2170.
do	" 20th		4 guns sent in to the trenches to relief 4 guns of the 138th Bde. M.G. Coy. Relief carried out at night. No casualties.	2170.
	" 21st		4 more guns sent in to the trenches to carry out indirect fire on tracks etc behind enemy lines. No casualties.	2170.
	" 22nd		All men not in the trenches working under R.E. Officer. 1. O.R. Casualty. Usual Indirect fire carried out by guns in the line.	2170.
	" 24th to 29th		Preliminary Bombardment for attack. 1 O.R. Casualty on the 24th. Machine Guns carried out indirect fire on tracks & dumps in rear of enemy lines. 2 guns in the front line played on gaps made by our Artillery in the enemy wire at intervals throughout the night. These guns were mounted on our front-line parapet & on only one occasion did they have to cease fire on account of enemy shelling. Intermittent shelling of our front & support lines throughout the day & night. Shelling of our front & support lines fairly heavy after smoke demonstrations. no casualties	2170.
	Night of 28/29		8 guns in the line relieved by the 8 guns in billets at POMMIER. No casualty. Weather very bad. C.T's well over the knees in water, mud very thick & heavy. no casualties	2170.
	June 29 & 30th		Preliminary Bombardment & Machine Gun fire as for the preceeding days. no casualties	2170.

H. Williston Lt.

Machine Gun Company, 139th Brigade.

To.

139th Inf. Brigade.

Herewith War Diary of the Company for month of July.

2/M Adams Lt.
for OC 139th Bde M G Coy

139th BRIGADE
MACHINE GUN
COMPANY.

No. .... to/A
Date... 2-8-16

July 1916.

WAR DIARY
or
INTELLIGENCE SUMMARY
(Erase heading not required.)

Army Form C. 2118

139th Brigade. Machine Gun Company

Place	Date 1916	Hour	Summary of Events and Information	Remarks and references to Appendices
FONQUEVILLERS	1st July		The Brigade attacked the enemy lines at GOMMECOURT in accordance with VII Corps Scheme. The 137th Brigade were attacking on our right. **Objective of the Brigade.** To capture and consolidate the enemy trenches FOREIGN, FORT & FONT, about the N.W corner of GOMMECOURT WOOD to their junction with OUSE Communication Trench and thence along this communication trench to its junction with the enemy's second line, along FOX trench and ORANGE communication trench through the LITTLE "Z" to our original front line. Copy of Operation Orders attached.	REF. Att: Map Map "A"
		1 p.m.	The guns moved off from the village to take up their allotted positions in RETRENCHMENT and the 1st SUPPORT LINE. ZERO hour was 7.30 a.m. The preliminary bombardment commenced at 6.25 a.m and lifted at 7-30 a.m. Smoke was discharged at 7.25 a.m and lasted for a period of 1 hour.	
		7-30 am	Infantry assault commenced. No 3 Section (2 guns) reached within 20 yds of the enemy front line but were unable to enter this line as it was then occupied by the enemy. These guns came into action from shell-holes and fired on enemy observed in front of GOMMECOURT WOOD. The smoke here was very thin. No 1 Section. 3 guns were known to have passed the enemy wire. Of these two were put out of action before coming into action and the third opened fire on the enemy from a shell hole. This gun had to be abandoned, later, but was first put out of action. The 4th gun was reported to have been seen lying in the enemy wire with the N.C.O in charge (casualty). All the men of this section who returned reported practically no smoke after passing our advanced front line.	

July 1916

WAR DIARY or INTELLIGENCE SUMMARY

Army Form C. 2118.

Vol 6

139th Brigade Machine Gun Company

Place	Date 1916	Hour	Summary of Events and Information	Remarks and references to Appendices

FONQUEVILLERS	1st July		**No. 2 Section.** Only three of these guns left our front line trench, the fourth getting stuck in the mud and got out of touch. Of the three guns that went over, one passed the advanced front line trench. Here the smoke was very thin and no Infantry were visible so the N.C.O. i/c ordered his gun to return. Only 2 men were left at this time. The other guns returned to the front line trench.
			
			 No. 4 Section. These guns were not sent across.
			
			 4 guns in Support. These guns moved forward into the front line trench and took up positions there. They were not sent across.
			
			 Casualties. 4 Officers. Capt. F.B. ROBINSON died of wounds. 3/7/16.
			                                 Lieut. G.F. GARDNER wounded. 1/7/16
			                                 2/Lieut. E.J. PEACH wounded & missing 1/7/16.
			                                 2/Lieut. W.R. CLAYTON wounded. 1/7/16.
			
			 50 O.R.
				2/1/a

do.	2nd July		Lt. H.C. WOLLASTON returned from Hospital and took over command of Company.	2/1/a
	2nd July	4.30 pm	Company relieved by the 138th Brigade Machine Gun Company and moved to huts at WARLINCOURT.	2/1/a
WARLINCOURT	3rd July	10 a.m	Company moved to billets in Divisional Reserve at SAULTY.	2/1/a
SAULTY	4th July 6th 8th July		Re-organizing and usual training carried out. 22 O.R. reinforcements received.	2/1/a
	10th July	11 a.m	Inspected by G.O.C. Division. Moved to new billetting area at BELLACOURT.	2/1/a

WAR DIARY or INTELLIGENCE SUMMARY

Army Form C. 2118.

July 1916.

139th Brigade Machine Gun Company

Place	Date	Hour	Summary of Events and Information	Remarks and references to Appendices
BELLACOURT	July 11th	1 p.m.	Took over machine gun positions occupied by the 166 Brigade Machine Gun Company. 8 guns put into the line. Sketch maps attached. No casualties. 137th Brigade on RIGHT. 56th Div. on LEFT.	See Map "B" 2170
	July 12th to July 17th		Indirect fire on enemy villages and tracks carried out during the night. Work in improving old and constructing new emplacements carried out. Very quiet - no casualties.	2170 2170
	July 18th		3 more guns put into the line in PARK LANE. Support line between OSIERS ST and COUTEREL ST. Front line between OSIER ST and DYKE ST.

Combined artillery and machine gun operations against enemy tracks, villages and roads liable to be used by transport. No Casualties.
Time - 11.52 p.m. to 12.12 a.m.
12.37 a.m. to 12.57 a.m.
1.25 a.m. to 1.45 a.m.
Retaliation negligible. | 2170 2170 |
| | July 19th to July 31st

July 29th | | Indirect fire carried out on enemy villages & tracks. Very quiet. Casualties Nil.
2 more guns put into the line. 1 in Support near PARK LANE. 1 in OSIERS FRONT LINE. 1 in each strong post. BOUNDARY, STARFISH, BURNT FARM & ORCHARD POST.
3 Officers arrived from Base and taken on strength.
 2 Lieut. W. H. HOFF.
 2 Lt. J. A. HODGE
 2 Lt. P. W. DEXTER | See Map "B" 2170 2170 2170 |
| | July 31st | | Lieut. J. L. PERCIVAL 6th SHERWOOD FORESTERS attached for duty. | 2170 |

OPERATION ORDERS
by
Capt: F.B.Robinson Commanding
139th Brigade Machine Gun Company

1. **GENERAL SCHEME OF ADVANCE.**

   12 Machine Gun will move forward in rear of the 4 wave of the attacking Battalions.
   These Guns will advance as follows:-
   No.3 Section with 2 Guns (under 2nd Lieut: Peach) with LEFT on Junction of OHIO and FORK.
   No.1 Section with 4 Guns (under Lieut: Gardner) with RIGHT on junction of OHIO and FORK.
   No.2 Section with 4 Guns (under 2nd Lieut: Clayton) with CENTRE on junction of OUSE and FOOD.
   No.4 Section with 2 Guns (under 2nd Lieut: Kemshall) with right reentrant of LITTLE "Z".

2. **NUMBERING OF GUNS**

   Guns will be numbered from RIGHT to LEFT from 1 to 12.
   No.3 Section   1 & 2.
   No.1 Section   3, 4, 5, & 6.
   No.2 Section   7, 8, 9, & 10.
   No.4 Section   11 & 12.

3. **TEMPORARY POSITIONS**

   The Guns will be placed in the following temporary positions.
   (a). No.3 Section Nos.1 & 2 Guns on RIGHT of FOOT TRENCH. If circumstances are favourable No.1 Gun will be placed in ORKNEY C.T. to anfilate FOREIGN, FORT, and FONT trenches.
   (b). No.1 Section. No.3 Gun in FOOT TRENCH on RIGHT of OHIO. No.4 & 5 Guns in FOOT TRENCH between OHIO and ORINOCO. No.6 Gun in FOWL TRENCH on LEFT of ORINOCO.
   (c). No.2 Section Nos.7 & 8 Guns in FOWL to RIGHT of OUSE No.9 Gun in FOX to LEFT of OUSE. No.10 Gun in ORANGE C.T. (joining FOX and FOOD) covering LEFT FRONT
   (d). No.4 Section Nos.11 & 12 Guns in LITTLE "Z".

4. **AFTER THE CAPTURE OF TRENCH FOREIGN, FORT and FONT.**

   Officers will reconnoitre and move their Guns to the following positions:-
   (a). No.3 Section Nos. 1 & 2 Guns in TRENCH on N.E. edge of GOMMECOURT WOOD.
   (b). No.1 Section No.3 Gun in FOREIGN TRENCH on RIGHT of OHIO. Nos. 4 & 5 Guns in FORT TRENCH. No.6 Gun in FONT TRENCH.
   (c). No.2 Section Nos.7 & 8 Guns in OUSE C.T. so as to be able to cover S.W. face of PIGEON WOOD.

5. **AMMUNITION**

   Each Gun will take forward 14 boxes of S.A.A. in belts.

6. **SUPPORT**

   The remaining 4 Guns will move up in rear of the 2nd wave of the 5th Battalion (under Lieut: T.H.F.Adams). Guns will be placed in dug-outs if available. An emplacement will be made for each Gun to be used in case of necessity.
   All spare men will be attached to this Section to carry surplus belt boxes.

7. **CASUALTIES**

   Estimated number of casualties will be forwarded to

(2)

Company H.Qrs.with (6th Battalion H.Qrs.) as soon as possible after moving up into positions, no difference will be made between killed, wounded or missing. This return will not necessarily be very accurate.

Signed:-

[signature]
Capt:
Commanding 139th Brigade
Machine Gun Company.

SECRET

Map showing Bellacourt, Grosville, Bretencourt, Blairville area.

REFERENCE
- ☐ = Headquarters Section Officer
- ▪ Maxim Gun Battle Emplacement
- ▪ Coy. H. Qrs
- ▪ S.A.A.
- • Listening Post.

SCALE — 1/5000

REFERENCE

SCALE 1:5000

2ⁿᵈ OBJECTIVE

2"

56ᵀᴴ DIVISION

FIGURES AND ——— DENOTES
TIME ARTILLERY FIRE LIFTS OFF TRENCH

SECRET

MAP "A"

138th Machine Gun Company

2nd Sept. 1916.

To

139th Brigade.

Herewith War diary for Aug. 1916.

H Palmer Capt.
Commanding 138th Machine Gun Coy.

AUG 1916.

WAR DIARY
or
INTELLIGENCE SUMMARY
(Erase heading not required.)

Army Form C. 2118

Vol 7
139th Machine Gun Company

Place	Date	Hour	Summary of Events and Information	Remarks and references to Appendices
Bellacourt	Aug 5 7.a.m.		2Lt A Hart 11th Gordon Highlanders arrived from base & taken on strength. 4 guns, one complete Section brought back into reserve in Bellacourt. Coy. dispositions as follows. 1 Section in reserve. 1 " " supporting posts. 2 " " line. Positions in Park Lane & Ravine abandoned.	
	10"		Capt Paterson H.S. arrived from 44th M.g Coy 15th Division & took over command of the Coy from this date.	
	26		Lt Percival left to attend Trench Mortar course at 3rd Army Trench Mortar School LIGNY St FLOCHEL	
	28		Roumania declared war on Austria.	
			Work done alternative emplacements made, trench in neighbourhood of all positions built up revetted etc improved, deep dug-outs being made by R.E. for each position. Anti gas blankets erected.	
			Situation Quiet, indirect fire carried out nightly on enemy villages & communications direct fire on the BLOCKHOUSE & enemy parapets. Approx number of rounds fired during month 63,250 Coy has been armed entirely with Vickers guns, Maxims being returned to Ordnance.	
			Casualties etc 2Lt Kempshall accidentally wounded see strength state dated 1/9/16 1 O.R. wounded	

1875 Wt. W593/826 1,000,000 4/15 J.B.C. & A. A.D.S.S./Forms/C. 2118.

H Paterson Capt.
Commanding 139th Machine Gun Coy

SEPT: 1916

WAR DIARY or INTELLIGENCE SUMMARY

(Erase heading not required.)

Army Form C. 2118.

Vol 8

139th Machine Gun Company

Place	Date	Hour	Summary of Events and Information	Remarks and references to Appendices
BELLACOURT	Sept 14		Lieut. H.C. WOOLASTON, 1/5th Sherwood Foresters, seconded to Machine Gun Corps, left for ENGLAND and struck off strength.	
			Transfers of 77 NCO's and men from 139 Infantry Brigade completed, bringing company up to establishment.	
			22 O.R. from Brigade remain attached.	
	Sept 17		2Lt A.M. HART admitted to Hospital, sick.	
	Sept 21	6.15 pm	Gun in front line destroyed by explosion of a heavy shell, which fell in front of loophole of No 2 battle emplacement.	
	Sept 21	11.30 pm	Two guns and teams placed at the disposal of 8th Sherwood Foresters to protect the flanks of a raiding party on ITALY SAP and front line. Teams composed as follows:— 1 N.C.O. } 3 gun numbers } armed with revolvers 1 rifleman attached from Infantry	
			Teams took up positions in shell holes under the near edge of enemy wire.	
	" 22	12.10 am	Shortly after trench was entered, an enemy machine gun opened fire from a sap to the right, and was quickly engaged and silenced by right flanking gun and 1 Lewis gun.	
		1.15 am	Teams returned safely, covering retirement of infantry.	
			Revolvers were found to be preferable to rifles for this operation.	
			2Lt A.M. HART returned from No 20 Casualty Clearing Station.	
	" 25	1 pm	Enemy fired 12 shells into neighbourhood of HQ billets. 1 Shell exploded in a billet and destroyed it. 4 men were killed.	
GROSVILLE	" 26	5 pm	Coy HQ's transferred from BELLACOURT to GROSVILLE, where safer billets are found.	
			WORK DONE 3 new emplacements constructed. Trenches at all positions repaired, revetted, and improved. Dug-out under construction at front line position of No 5 gun at head of ROADWAY. Anti-gas measures in trenches being carried out.	

SEPT. 1916. (II)

WAR DIARY or INTELLIGENCE SUMMARY

(Erase heading not required.)

Army Form C. 2118.

139th Machine Gun Company

Place	Date	Hour	Summary of Events and Information	Remarks and references to Appendices
			SITUATIONS.	

Quiet; 2 emplacements damaged by shell fire, and 1 gun destroyed. These losses have been made good.

Indirect fire carried out nightly on enemy villages and communications.

Direct fire on enemy parapets and gaps in wire.

Approx: number of rounds fired during month - 85,000 rounds.

Two rifle batteries are in position and are being fired regularly on selected targets.

CASUALTIES etc.

 4 O.R. killed by shell-fire.   25.9.16

Wounded. 1 O.R. by rifle bullet   5.9.16
    2 O.R. by concussion of shell. 21.9.16.

H Paterson Capt

Commanding 139th M.G. Company.

October 1916.

WAR DIARY
or
INTELLIGENCE SUMMARY
(Erase heading not required.)

Army Form C. 2118.
Vol 9

139th Machine Gun Company
(46th Division)

Place	Date	Hour	Summary of Events and Information	Remarks and references to Appendices
GROSVILLE	9-6ct	4 am	2 Guns and teams placed at the disposal of 7th Sherwood Foresters to protect the flanks of a Raiding Party, posted on either side of BLAMONT - BLAIREVILLE ROAD. Neither gun was engaged. Casualties, 2 O.R. slightly wounded by splinters from T.M. Bombs.	
	7th	—	2/Lt A.M. HART left for ENGLAND on duty.	
	29th	3 pm.	Company was relieved in "D" Sector trenches by 90th Machine Gun Coy.	
	30th	—	Company moved from GROSVILLE into billets at SUS ST LEGER.	

WORK DONE

2 new indirect firing emplacements constructed. Trenches at all positions repaired, and drained. Revetting work continued. Front line dug-out at RANSART ROADWAY completed, and team moved in. Anti-gas measures at all positions perfected.

SITUATIONS

Quiet. Hostile shelling slightly increased from previous month. Emplacements (alternative) in Centre Sector located by enemy during daylight firing, & shelled; - no damage done.
Indirect fire carried out nightly on enemy villages & communications.
Direct fire by day & night on enemy parapets and gaps in wire.
2 Rifle Batteries fired regularly on selected targets.
Approximate number of rounds fired during month, — 95,000 rounds

CASUALTIES 2 O.R. slightly wounded (1 at duty)

H. Paterson Capt
Commanding 139th M.G. Company

November 1916

WAR DIARY
or
INTELLIGENCE SUMMARY
(Erase heading not required.)

Army Form C. 2118

139th Machine Gun Company

Vol 10

Place	Date	Hour	Summary of Events and Information	Remarks and references to Appendices
SUS-ST-LEGER	1st	—	Company moved from SUS-ST-LEGER into billets at CANELEUX.	
CANELEUX	3rd	—	Company moved from CANELEUX into billets at HIERMONT.	
HIERMONT	6th	—	Company moved from HIERMONT into billets at NEUVILLE D'ONEX. Lieut. T.H.F. ADAMS and 2 O.R. proceeded to attend Course. Advanced M.G.S. CAMIERS commencing 6th inst.	
NEUVILLE D'ONEX	11th	—	Company moved from NEUVILLE D'ONEX into billets at HIERMONT.	
	21st	—	Ceremonial Parade at HIERMONT.	
HIERMONT	22	—	Company moved from HIERMONT into billets at ST. ACHEUL.	
ST ACHEUL	23	—	Company moved from ST ACHEUL into billets at OCCOCHES.	
	23	—	Lieut. F.W.N. FINLAYSON arrived from 154 M.G. Coy and taken on Strength of Company as 2nd in Command.	
OCCOCHES	25	—	Company moved from OCCOCHES into billets at WARLUZEL.	
WARLUZEL	29	—	Capt. H.S. PATERSON admitted Hospital (sick). 1 Officer and 64 O.R. proceeded to X Roads N.28.C.25.05 for work under R.E.s.	
"	30	—	Company issued with new pattern Box Respirator & fitted with same. Programme of Training. 10 minutes Run, Physical Training. Advanced Gun Drill. Use of Elevating & Traversing Dials. Theory of Indirect Fire. Lectures by O.C. on "Tactical handling of M.G's." Night Operations.	

F.W.N. Finlayson
Lieut.
for. O.C. 139th Machine Gun Company.

December 1916.

WAR DIARY or INTELLIGENCE SUMMARY
(Erase heading not required.)

Army Form C. 2118

Vol XI

139th Machine Gun Company

Place	Date	Hour	Summary of Events and Information	Remarks and references to Appendices
FONQUEVILLERS	5th	—	Company took over trenches from the 147 Machine Gun Company	
"	8th	—	Lieut. N.H.B. REZIN granted leave to SCOTLAND from 8/12/16 to 20/12/16.	
"	9th	6.P.M	No 3 Gun was shelled with heavy Trench Mortars, team shelter being destroyed	
"	11th	—	Enemy very active with 5.9s round No 1 emplacement. Heavy and Light Trench Mortar activity by the enemy round No 3 emplacement.	
"	13th	11 AM	No 1 Position taken over by 93rd Machine Gun Company.	
"	"	—	2/Lt A.M. HART proceeded on Course of Instruction at Infantry School, ST AMAND.	
"	"	—	40 Reinforcements arrived from Base Depot and taken on strength of Coy.	
"	15th	—	No 2 Gun Position was shelled with 4.2's, overhead covering being damaged.	
"	16th	9 AM	No 1 Gun came into action at MOULIN DETROIT.	
"	17th	—	2 O.R. reinforcements arrived from Base Depot and taken on strength of Coy.	
"	18th	—	Nos. 7, 8, and 9 Gun Positions heavily shelled during forenoon, No 7 emplacement and dug-out received direct hits. Trench at entrance to No 9 emplacement blown in.	
"	20th	—	Occupation of new positions at "FORT DICK" (No 5), SAILLY ROAD POST (No 6), SNIPERS SQUARE (No 10), and E.21.b.64 (No 11). The following positions were evacuated :- Nos. 5, 8, 10 and 11. Nos. 8 & 9 positions were shelled during 8.30 p.m. and 9.30 p.m. No 8 emplacement receiving a direct hit, slightly damaging the tripod. No 3 Position was Trench Mortared. FORT DICK Gun team had to wear their gas masks during "Z" operations owing to Gas shells fired at batteries in their vicinity.	
"	23	—	Capt. H.S. PATERSON returned to duty from Hospital.	

December 1916.

WAR DIARY or INTELLIGENCE SUMMARY

(Erase heading not required.)

Army Form C. 2118

139th Machine Gun Company

Place	Date	Hour	Summary of Events and Information	Remarks and references to Appendices
FONQUEVILLERS	25th		Capt. H.S. PATERSON admitted to Hospital (sick)	
	26th		No 2 Position and entrance to dug-out was blown in (by a heavy shell, probably a 5.9)	
	29th		Lieut W.H. HOFF proceeded on Course of Instruction.	
	27	2.55 a/m	Enemy bombarded our CENTRE SECTOR.	
	&	3.40 a/m		
	31		2/Lt. A.M. HART returned from Course of Instruction.	

Casualties.
No 43681 Pte JOHNSON. A.W. Shrapnel wounds to head & arms. (11/12/16).
No 42664 Pte DALGLEISH R. One eye knocked out and other believed to be affected (19/12/16).

Work Done.
Open emplacement in Support Line for No 3 Gun. Temporary "Indirect fire" emplacement built at E.26.d.20.45. Trenches revetted, dug-outs repaired and strengthened. Shelter in SNIPERS SQUARE made. Improvements to Gun Positions. Gun Position (No 1) built at MOULIN DETROIT. Sanitary improvements carried out. SAILLY ROAD POST position made, and cover for S.A.A. New open emplacements built at E.21.b.50 & E.21.b.64. Trenches cleaned and floorboards laid.

Transfers
32 O.R. attached to this Company from Battns transferred to the Machine Gun Corps (139th Machine Gun Company). with effect from 19/12/16.
2/Lieut R.J.C. SHIPLEY transferred from 33 M.G. Coy and taken on strength of this Company. (3/12/16).

Commanding 139th M. Gun Company.
/Lieut.

Jany. 1917

WAR DIARY or INTELLIGENCE SUMMARY

Army Form C. 2118

139th Machine Gun Company. M.G.C.

Vol XII

Place	Date	Hour	Summary of Events and Information	Remarks and references to Appendices
FONQUEVILLERS	1st		Vicinity of No 4 Gun heavily shelled by 77 m.m. shells.	
	6th		Old Emplacement at No. 3 Gun Position hit by a 4.2 shell.	
	11th		Back entrance to Officer's dug-out at No. 1. Gun (MOULIN DETROIT) blown in by a 5.9 shell.	
	12th		Transport lines shelled, 4 mules being killed and 7 seriously injured.	
	15th		2 Lieut. P.W. DEXTER posted to 119 M.G. Coy and struck off strength of this Company	
	16th		3 Reinforcements arrived from Base Depot and taken on strength of Coy.	
			Lieut. W.H.B. REZIN returned to duty from Course of Instruction.	
	17th		Capt. H.S. PATERSON evacuated to ENGLAND (Sick) and struck off strength of Coy.	
	19th		Co-operation with Divisional Artillery on following targets - Enfilading KITE COPSE - COMMECOURT ROAD, COMMECOURT VILLAGE, COMMECOURT WOOD, Railway at K.4.b., and PIGEON WOOD.	
			Lieut. F.C. HOLDEN taken on strength of Coy. from Base Depot.	
	21st		No 10. Position was heavily shelled during early afternoon.	
			2 Lieut J.A. HODGE proceeded on short leave to U.K.	
	23rd		Lieut. T.H.F. ADAMS returned to duty from short leave to U.K.	
	24th		Lieut. R.J.C. SHIPLEY proceeded on Course of Instruction at GAUDIEMPRE.	
	25th		No. 1 dug-out blown in, some 40 shells were fired round this position, probably 4.2 shells	
	28		Lieut. F.W.N. FINLAYSON proceeded on short leave to U.K.	
	29		Enemy shelled No 1 Gun Position and dug-out with 4.2 & 5.9 shells.	
	30		Enemy again shelled No 1 Gun Position.	
			Casualties.	
			72072 Pte SHAW. J Killed (died of shell shock) 24/1/17.	
			72070 " TURNER A. Wounded (shrapnel wound in leg) 31/1/17.	
			Approx number of rounds expended during month - 33,350.	2H.F Adams Lt ft. 139 M.G Coy

Jany 1917

WAR DIARY
or
INTELLIGENCE SUMMARY
(Erase heading not required.)

139th Machine Gun Coy.

Army Form C. 2118

Place	Date	Hour	Summary of Events and Information	Remarks and references to Appendices
FONQUEVILLERS	1/1/17 to 31/1/17		**Work done** Sandbag wall built up in old dug-out at No. 8 Gun. Alternative Emplacement in COLONEL'S WALK rebuilt. No. 8 Gun Buttress in dug-out completed. No. 9 Gun, Shelter for Ammunition. Traverse built at Alternative position in COLONEL'S WALK. Bank in front of No. 4 Gun raised. Radial mountings put at Nos. 1 & 6 Positions. Sap leading to No. 3 Gun revetted. Cellars at Coy. H.Qrs. strengthened. "Frog" at No. 5 Gun completed. Trench deepened and boards laid at No. 5 Gun. Roof of No. 1 dug-out repaired. ROTTON ROW revetted and floorboards laid. Fixed Pivot mounting in SNIPERS SQUARE. Traverse at No. 2 Gun made. Assisting R.E.'s at No. 8 & 9 dug-outs. Emplacement at FORT DICK revetted. Trench at SNIPERS SQUARE sandbagged. Excavating ground for dug-out at FORT DICK. Trenches drained, revetted and repaired.	

2/Lt Aclaud Lt.
f.c. 139th M.G.Coy

Feby 1917

WAR DIARY or INTELLIGENCE SUMMARY
(Erase heading not required.)

Army Form C. 2118

46 Division
139th Machine Gun Company

Vol 13

Place	Date	Hour	Summary of Events and Information	Remarks and references to Appendices
FONQUEVILLERS	1st	—	Lieut. F.W.N. FINLAYSON to be acting Capt. with effect from 14/12/16 (Authority AG's list No 120a/27/1/17).	
	1st	12 Noon	139 M.G. Coy relieved the 2 Guns of 138 M.G. Coy in new sector under arrangements of Coy Commander.	
	2nd	4 P.M.	Brigade front extended Northwards to Trench 60 (inclusive). No 4 Gun moved from ROBINSON'S LANE to new front line position at top of CRAWL BOYS LANE and No 10 Gun to GENDARMERIE. The Gun at SNIPERS SQUARE detailed to fall back to No 5 Strong Post if necessary.	
			About 30 shells were fired near No 1 Gun during afternoon and evening. Enemy M.G. fired in village between 8 and 9 P.M.	
	3rd		Lieut. W.H. HOFF returned from Course of Instruction at AUXI-LE-CHATEAU.	
	4th	7 A.M.	Enemy Transport clearly heard behind GOMMECOURT.	
	6th		Lieut. E.B. WOODFORDE proceeded on Course of Instruction at AUXI-LE-CHATEAU commencing 7/2/17.	
	9th	11-Midnight	Enemy M Gun fired into Village from direction of GOMMECOURT PARK also another Gun fired into SUNKEN ROAD at CALVAIRE about the same hour.	
	10th		2/Lieut. J.A. HODGE returned from short leave to U.K. (granted extension of 7 days sick leave). Enemy retaliated on our M. Gun which was firing indirect. Enemy M. Gun fired on ARTILLERY CROSS RDS between 6-8 P.M.	
	12th		2/Lieut. H.W. BROWN and 3 O.R. reinforcements arrived from Base Depot and taken on strength of Coy.	
			Lieut. R.J.C. SHIPLEY returned from Course of Instruction at GAUDIEMPRE.	
	16th		During enemy shelling several tear shells dropped round No 9 Gun, tear shells also experienced at No 3, SNIPERS SQUARE and No 9 Guns between 1-30 A.M. and 1-50 A.M. A few trench mortars fell near No 2 Gun during the night. New dugouts for No 8 & 9 Gun teams occupied at night.	
	17th		Lieut. W.H. HOFF admitted Hospital suffering from effects of Gas (shells).	
	18th		Capt. F.W.N. FINLAYSON returned from short leave to U.K. (granted extension of 7 days sick leave).	
	19th		Brigade Front taken over by 138th Brigade. Our Machine Guns remained in with the 138th Brigade.	
	20th		2/Lieut C.F.O.G. FORBES transferred to Coldstream Guards Special Reserve U.K. and struck off strength.	
	21st		A few Gas shells were fired into THORPE STREET and FORT DICK between 6-7 P.M.	

FWN Finlayson /Capt.

Feb 1917
2.
46 Division
139th Machine Gun Company

WAR DIARY or INTELLIGENCE SUMMARY

Army Form C. 2118

(Erase heading not required.)

Place	Date	Hour	Summary of Events and Information	Remarks and references to Appendices
FONQUEVILLERS	22nd	—	4. O.R. Reinforcements arrived from Base Depot and taken on Strength of Company.	
	23rd	—	Enemy shelled FONQUEVILLERS at irregular intervals throughout the night.	
	24th	—	Very quiet night. Enemy M.G. fire intermittent during night.	
	25th	—	2/Lieut. W. BLYTH and 1. O.R. reinforcement arrived from Base Depot and taken on Strength. 2/Lieut. J.A. HODGE and 2. O.R. proceeded to CAMIERS on Course of Instruction commencing 26/2/17. Enemy Machine Gun in the "Z" was active during night.	
	26th	—	Enemy sent up red rockets between 5-30 - 6-0 a.m. along front line from PIGEON WOOD to GOMMECOURT PARK.	
	27th	—	Enemy evacuated their front line trenches, GOMMECOURT VILLAGE, and GOMMECOURT PARK.	
"	"	8-0 P.M.	A good many gas shells were fired into the village in the vicinity of the SHRINE.	
	1/2/17 - 28/2/17		WORK DONE. Dugouts for Nos. 8 & 9 Guns constructed under supervision of R.E's. Repaired entrance to "E" Indirect Fire position. Repaired No. 1 Gun Position. Covered roof of No 1 Gun dug-out. Enlarged emplacement for No 12 Gun. 6 Emplacements made on SAILLY ROAD. Building up partition for Officers' dug-out at No 1. Gun. 6 Emplacements made in NAMELESS ROAD. Deepened MILL STREET near Gun position. Deepened trench to SNIPERS SQUARE Gun and alternative emplacement. Emplacements for Nos. 10, 11, and 12 Guns rebuilt. Gun emplacement at No 8 Gun. Alternative emplacement for No 7 Gun.	
			CASUALTIES. No. 24274 Pte WYLD S. gas (shell) 17/2/17. Approx. number of rounds expended during month. 39,150.	

March 1917

WAR DIARY or INTELLIGENCE SUMMARY

(Erase heading not required.)

Vol 14

139th Machine Gun Company

Army Form C. 2118

Place	Date	Hour	Summary of Events and Information	Remarks and references to Appendices
FONQUEVILLERS	1st	-	Company Battle H. Qrs ARTILLERY CROSS ROADS. FONQUEVILLERS. Enemy Machine Guns were very active. They appeared to be firing on barrage lines but could not be detected. 2 Guns took up positions in GOMMECOURT. 4 O.R. reinforcements arrived from Base Depot and taken on strength of Company.	
	2nd		4 Guns took up positions in Sub-Section HANNESCHAMPS.	
	3rd		4 Guns relieved the 2 Guns in GOMMECOURT.	
	4th		Enemy evacuated PIGEON WOOD, The "Z" and Little "Z".	
	5th		2 Guns took up Positions in BIEZ WOOD. During the day the enemy retired to a line EAST of BIEZ WOOD and EAST and NORTH of RETTEMOY FARM. This line probably runs along the hedge running NORTH of KITE COPSE.	
	8th		4 Guns in HANNESCHAMPS Sub-section relieved by the 138th M.G. Coy. 139th Infantry Brigade front extended from S.E. corner of BIEZ WOOD to E. 23 d. 7.9 (Ref. Fong 1/10000)	
	9th		6. O.R. reinforcements arrived from Base Depot and taken on strength of Coy.	
	10th		Lieut. W.H. HOFF returned to Duty from Hospital. About 6-30 pm enemy (about 30) were seen approaching our line by communication trench running between RETTEMOY GRABEN and RETTEMOY FARM. They were dispersed by our M.G. fire.	
	11th		Lieut. W.H.B. REZIN admitted Hospital suffering from effects of Gas (shells).	
	12th		5 Guns conformed to the Artillery programme with barrage fire on BOCQUOY GRABEN.	
	13th		Battle Headquarters moved from FONQUEVILLERS to dug-out (SELBSTRETTER) in old German 3rd line. Gun at BRAYELLE GRABEN withdrawn to PIGEON WOOD owing to heavy hostile trench mortar and Artillery fire.	
	15th		Lieut. E.B. WOODFORDE rejoined Unit from Course of Instruction at AUXI-LE-CHATEAU.	
	17th		Company relieved by 138th M.G. Coy. relief proceeded to THORPE ST. via WESSEX WALK to SOUASTRE	
SOUASTRE.	18th		Lieut. W.H.B. REZIN returned to Duty from Hospital.	
	19th		2/Lieut J.A. HODGE rejoined Unit from Course of Instruction at CAMIERS. 2/Lieut A.T. JONES arrived from Base Depot and taken on strength of Company.	
	20th		Company moved from SOUASTRE into Huts at BAYENCOURT (Map ref. J. 16 a.)	

O.C. 139th M.G. Coy.

March 1917.

WAR DIARY or INTELLIGENCE SUMMARY
(Erase heading not required.)

Army Form C. 2118

139th Machine Gun Company.

Place	Date	Hour	Summary of Events and Information	Remarks and references to Appendices
BAYENCOURT	21st		Lieut R.J. SHIPLEY admitted to Hospital (sick).	
	23rd		Company moved from BAYENCOURT into new billets at CONTAY.	
CONTAY	24th		Company moved from CONTAY into new billets at VILLERS BOCAGE.	
VILLERS BOCAGE	25th		Company moved from VILLERS BOCAGE into new billets at ST FUSCIEN.	
	24th		2/Lieut D.E.L. JONES arrived from Base Depot and taken on strength of Company.	
ST FUSCIEN	26th		Company moved from ST FUSCIEN into new billets at CLAIRY-SAULCHOIX.	
	27th		Company entrained at BACOUEL STATION at 6.0 p.m.	
	28th		Company detrained at CHOCQUES STATION at 4-45 p.m. and proceed to billets at LIGNY-LEZ-AIRE.	
LIGNY-LEZ-AIRE			Lieut R.J.C. SHIPLEY evacuated Divisional Area and struck off strength of Company.	
	29th		Lieut C.D. POUND arrived from Base Depot and taken on strength of Company.	
	30th		6 O.R reinforcements arrived from Base Depot and taken on strength of Company.	

Casualties during month = 1. officer Lieut W.H.B REZIN gas shells (since rejoined Unit) and 9.O.R.

No. 46317. Pte REID R.H. shrapnel wound of leg and arm 4/3/17.
No. 24236 L/Cpl. JOHNSON G.F. gas. 12/3/17 since rejoined Unit.
No. 24277 Pte MELTON B gas. 12/3/17 do.
No. 24253 Pte SPONAGE G gas. 12/3/17 do.
No. 72082 Pte PRATT E. gas. 12/3/17 do.
No. 24231 Pte ELLISON H. gas. 12/3/17
No. 16410 Pte SEWELL J gas. 12/3/17
No. 3379 Pte DUGUID J. shrapnel wound of ankle 13/3/17
No. 68403 Pte CHRISTOPHER H. shrapnel wound of knee and shoulder.

Approximate number of rounds expended during month = 22,850.

Programme of Work whilst in Rest billets =
Indication and Recognition of Targets.
Use of ground and cover.
Oaraused Gun Drill and Oaraused Action Drill
Respirator Drill. Tactical Schemes.

O.C. 139th M.G. Company.

April 1917

WAR DIARY or INTELLIGENCE SUMMARY

Army Form C. 2118

139th MACHINE GUN COMPANY M.G.C.

Vol 15

Place	Date	Hour	Summary of Events and Information	Remarks and references to Appendices
LIGNY-LEZ-AIRE	1st		Company in Rest Billets. Lieut T.H.F. ADAMS transferred to M.G.T.C. GRANTHAM under Authority A.G's A/23232.	
	2nd		1 O.R. reinforcement from Base Depot taken on strength of Company.	
	5th		Lieut R.J.C. SHIPLEY returned to Duty from Hospital. Capt F.W.N. FINLAYSON evacuated to U.K. and struck off strength of Company.	
	9th		March Exercise carried out by all Units of the Division (except Train, M+S). One Section of this Company included in Vanguard, and marched after 5th Battn S Foresters, rest of Company included in Mainguard – Dress full marching order.	
CHOCQUES	13th		Company moved into new billets CHOCQUES. Lieut W.A.B. REZIN took over Command of Coy from Lieut E.B. WOODFORDE.	
NOEUX-LES-MINES	14th		Company moved into new billets at NOEUX-LES-MINES.	
	16th		2/Lieut D.A. HODGE wounded (shrapnel wound of leg) and struck off strength of Company.	
ANGRES	19th		Company moved to ANGRES.	
	20th		Company relieved 73rd M.G. Coy in trenches (LIEVIN) front M.29.a.2.1.15 M.23.d.6.6. (Map Ref. LENS 1/10,000 and 36B 1/20,000) relief complete 10 P.M. ~~Coy H.Qrs M.28.c.99~~. 6 Guns Front line, 2 Guns Support, 2 Gun Reserve. Coy H.Qrs ANGRES	
LIEVIN	21st		Lt C.R. FAY arrived from 178 Divisional Company and took over Command. Company H.Qrs moved to M.28.c.9.9.	
	23rd		Enemy Artillery active during day and night. ~~S.M. Guns H Coy co-operated in frontal attack on HILL 65 – FOSS 3 with Indirect and flanking fire~~	
	24th		Enemy M.G. fired all night on LIEVIN-LENS Road. Company H.Qrs moved to M.28.a.4.6. 1 O.R. reinforcement arrived from Base Depot & taken on strength	
	26th		Several heavy explosions observed in LENS about 14 Central. On evening and early morning of 27inst heavy enemy barrage from CRAZY to CHATEAU (M.23.d.5.7.) 1 O.R. reinforcement arrived from Base Depot.	
	27th		Flame shell explosions bursting on ST. PIERRE at 10.30 P.M. Armour piercing Field Gun Shell fell close to Gun position in M.23.b.90.95.	
	27/28		5th Sherwood Foresters carried out a Raid with about 50 men against enemy trenches and houses on HILL 65. Our M. Guns arranged a barrage in conjunction with Artillery	

April 1917

2.

WAR DIARY or INTELLIGENCE SUMMARY
(Erase heading not required.)

Army Form C. 2118

139th MACHINE GUN COMPANY

Place	Date	Hour	Summary of Events and Information	Remarks and references to Appendices
LIEVIN	28th		At 8.40 P.M. a direct hit was obtained by enemy on Gun Emplacement in CRAZY, no damage was done to Gun or tripod, as it occurred just at the time of relief, when the Gun and tripod were dismounted.	
	29th		Gas projectors about BOIS-de-RIAMOUNT were fired, our M. Guns covered the discharge by bursts of fire on enemy communication trenches from 11.25 – 11.55 P.M.	
	30th		Company relieved by the 137th M.G. Coy and proceeded Rest billets at BULLY GRENAY.	

Approx. No of rounds fired during Month – 16,250.

Casualties:-

2/Lieut J.A. HODGE 16/4/17 (Shrapnel wound of leg)
No 46695 Pte BARNES H. 22/4/17 (Shrapnel wound of foot)
No 24242 L/Cpl BENNETT A. 23/4/17 (wound of scalp)
No 57979 Pte ATKINSON W 23/4/17 (wounds of arm and legs)
No 36421 " CONNOLLY D 23/4/17 (Killed)
No 24219 " DEMPSTER E.A 23/4/17 (Killed)
No 43059 " SAXTON E.D. 23/4/17 (wounded)
No 35347 " SCHORAH T. 23/4/17 (wounded)
No 58369 " BAILEY J. 23/4/17 (wounded)
No 43509 " ANDERSON J. 27/4/17 (slightly wounded)
No 24228 Sgt WATSON J.H. 29/4/17 (wounded, glass in eye)

2 O.R. No 72078 Pte NASS H and No 31196 Pte SWIFT J slightly wounded 23/4/17 but remained at Duty

Programme of Work while in Rest billets

Physical Training, Advanced Gun Drill, Indication and Recognition of Targets, Use of Ground and Cover, Tactical Schemes, Gun Drill with box respirators. and firing on Range.

C.R. Fay Lieut.
O.C. 139th M.G. Company

May 1917

WAR DIARY or INTELLIGENCE SUMMARY
(Erase heading not required.)

Army Form C. 2118.

139th Machine Gun Company

Vol 16

Place	Date	Hour	Summary of Events and Information	Remarks and references to Appendices
BULLY GRENAY	1st		Company in Rest billets at BULLY GRENAY	Map Ref. BULLY GRENAY LENS 1/10,000 and 36.b. 1/20,000
	"		2 Lieut A.M HART & 10 O.R. proceeded on Course of Instruction to "C" Battery Anti-aircraft	
	2nd		Lieut. H.H.B. REZIN proceeded on Course of Instruction to Central Corps.	
ST PIERRE	6th		Company relieved the 138th M.G Coy in the trenches at ST PIERRE. The Right Sector being occupied by a Section of the 178th M.G Coy.	
			Major H.D. MATSON arrived from Base Depot and took over Command of Company.	
			Left Sector. Enemy Artillery and Trench Mortars active during the night.	
			Right Sector. Heavy shelling on this Sector during the night.	
			Support. About 11.15 pm enemy obtained a hit on one of our bomb stores in LOOS, causing fire and continual explosions until 3.30 A.M.	
	7th		Enemy working party seen at work about NEILSON TRENCH.	
			7 O.R. reinforcements arrived from Base Depot and taken on strength of Company.	
			No 67016 Pte R. BERRIMAN awarded Military Medal.	
	8th		Enemy Artillery and Trench Mortars quiet during day, but very active during night.	
			Lieut C.R FAY returned to 178 M.G Coy and struck off strength of Company.	
	10th		Enemy shelled houses in N.7.a. and also burst heavy shrapnel in vicinity of MUSIC TRENCH on three occasions.	
	12th		2 Lieut. A.M HART & 8 O.R. returned from Course of Instruction (1 O.R. becoming casualty 1 O.R. sent to Rest Camp)	
	13th		Lieut R. PAGE arrived from 16th M.G Coy and taken on strength of Company as 2nd i/c	
	14th		17 O.R reinforcements arrived from Base Depot and taken on strength of Company.	
			Gun at N.1.a. 10.05 was damaged by shrapnel about 10.40 pm	
	15th	5.30 am	Dugout at N.1.a 35.00 hit by shell on top of entrance causing casualties	

May 1917

WAR DIARY or INTELLIGENCE SUMMARY

(Erase heading not required.)

Army Form C. 2118.

139th Machine Gun Company

Place	Date	Hour	Summary of Events and Information	Remarks and references to Appendices
ST. PIERRE.	15th		Enemy M.G. fire round concrete emplacement at M.6.d.30.35 more persistent than usual during the night, also down MUSIC TRENCH.	Map Ref. LENS 1/10,000 36 & 1/20,000
	17th		Quiet. The effects of lachrymatory shells on LOOS between 4.0 PM and 5.0 PM were felt in MUSIC TRENCH, and ~~one Gun in M.12.a.85.70~~	
	18th		Barrage fire on Gap in enemy wire (in conjunction with Artillery) by 4 Guns in MUSIC TRENCH and one Gun in M.12.a.85.70.	
	19th		During reconnaissance at 4.30 A.M. Gaps in wire in front of NASH ALLEY were seen to be still open. MUSIC TRENCH was shelled with H.E. but no alteration was made for barrage fire. Detached Gun team ordered for Duty with 7th S. Foresters. The 178 M.G. Coy only hold one position in the Divisional line i.e. M.5.c.3.0. Anti-aircraft Gun at M.16.b.6.6. has accordingly been moved to M.10.5.5 with Reserve Section.	
BULLY GRENAY			Company relieved by the 137 M.G. Coy and returned to Rest billets at BULLY GRENAY. Lieut. E.B. WOODFORDE granted short leave to U.K. from 19/5/17 - 29/5/17. Lieut. N.H. HOFF & 1 OR proceeded on Course of Instruction to CAMIERS.	
	20th		9 OR reinforcements arrived from Base Depot and took on strength of Company.	
	23rd		2 Lieut. N. BLYTH & 2 OR proceeded to Rest Camp, BOULOGNE.	
LIEVIN.	25th		Company relieved the 138th M.G. Coy in the trenches at LIEVIN. 2 Guns ordered to new positions to assist the 137th M.G. Coy.	
	26th		2 Guns temporarily placed in positions at M.17.b.28.20 and M.17.b.47.27 were returned to their original emplacements. Enemy Trench Mortars were active during the night particularly round CROOK & CRAZY Redoubts. Gas was felt at M.23.d.52.50 and M.17.a.85.00. Box Respirators were worn. Lieut. C.D. POUND admitted to Hospital (sick).	

May 1917

WAR DIARY
or
INTELLIGENCE SUMMARY
(Erase heading not required.)

Army Form C. 2118.

139th Machine Gun Company

Place	Date	Hour	Summary of Events and Information	Remarks and references to Appendices
LIEVIN.	27th		Enemy M.G. and Trench Mortars active during night. Cloud gas sent over by enemy at 7.30 pm effects felt in M.23.a. 3. N.C.O's. reinforcements arrived from Base Depot and took on strength of Company.	MAP Ref LENS 1/10,000 36 c 1/20,000
	28th		Gun Position at M.23.a.25.65. was shelled, and Position at M.17.c.80.47 swept by cross fire of 2 Machine Guns.	
	29th		Heavy Trench Mortaring round position at M.23.b.90.05. At 7.0 pm hostile aeroplane flew close to A.A Gun at M.23.a.50.71 and on Gun opening fire, dropped 3 lights. This resulted in the position being bombarded with 77 mm shells.	
	30th		At 12.30 AM and 1.45 AM Sector heavily bombarded. Lieut E.B. WOODFORDE returned from leave to U.K. Barrage fire in conjunction with Artillery on Abode and Advance trenches from Fire Gun position. No retaliation ensued from this bombardment. Enemy M.G. showed great activity.	
	31st		Heavy shelling reported on Left round CITÉ ST AMÉ. Trench Mortars active on Right. Gas, probably from Trench Mortars felt at 1.0 A.M. (1/6/17). Considerable movement was observed within the enemy's lines at N.19.b.70.80. Casualties during Month:— 43681. Pte. JOHNSON A.W. (wounded) 6/5/17. 81644. " BARNES. F.R. (wounded) 10/5/17. 24960. " CLATWORTHY H.H. (wounded) 11/5/17. 35277. " STEWART. J. (wounded) 15/5/17. 30837 " HUNT. M. (wounded) 15/5/17, since died of wounds. Approx. Number of rounds expended during month:— 80,200 rounds. A.A. Guns fired 10,250 rounds.	

May 1917

WAR DIARY
or
INTELLIGENCE SUMMARY
(Erase heading not required.)

Army Form C. 2118.

139th Machine Gun Company

Place	Date	Hour	Summary of Events and Information	Remarks and references to Appendices
LIEVIN			<u>Work Done</u> ST. PIERRE Trenches. Improvement of Emplacement in M.5.d.4.1. Gun Position and dug-out in MUSIC TRENCH improved and strengthened. New Position built at M.11.b.50.70. Anti-Aircraft Gun mounted at M.12.a.3.5. New emplacement at M.6.d.3.2. New emplacement dug at N.1.a.35.00, and deepening existing emplacement. Repairing and strengthening of trenches. Construction of shrapnel proof shelter for Gun at M.6.d.3.2. LIEVIN Trenches. Overhead cover constructed for emplacement at M.23.d.53.50. Position Constructed at M.28.d.70.20. Shelter trench dug and sand bagged at position M.17.d.85.00. Brick roofing placed on emplacement at M.23.d.53.50, and fresh struts put in. <u>Programme of Training while in Rest Billets</u>. C.O's Inspection each Morning at 9.A.M. Physical Training, Use of Clinometers, Bomb Throwing, Gas Drill. Gun Drill with Box Respirators. Firing on Range Butts. Lectures by Officers on "Maintenance of Discipline" "The Protection of M.Gs in House Warfare" "Duties of sentries" "Barrage".	MAP Ref. LENS 1/10,000 36.c/20,000

J.D. Mabson Major.
Commanding 139th M.G. Coy.

June 1917

WAR DIARY
or
INTELLIGENCE SUMMARY
(Erase heading not required.)

Army Form C. 2118.

139th Machine Gun Company

Map Ref. 36.C.S.W.1.

Place	Date	Hour	Summary of Events and Information	Remarks and references to Appendices
LIEVIN	1/6/17		Company in trenches at LIEVIN. Lieut. W.H.B. REBIN rejoined from Course of Instruction. Hostile M.G. reported at FOSSE 3. enfilading Road M.34.a.5.4 – M.35.c.75.60. Enemy Artillery active.	
	2nd		Normal during night. Very large fire observed burning in LENS about 11.15 p.m.	
	3rd		Lieut R. PAGE proceeded on Course of Instruction. Enemy Aircraft heard over LIEVIN at 10.45 P.M and 12.5 am. Two Vickers Guns placed in position S edge of BOIS de RIAMONT by 12.45 p.m. Barraged against projected counter attack. Firing was restricted owing to close conditions of Infantry fighting. On receipt of information that Canadians had withdrawn from POWER STATION, these Guns were brought back to their original positions. Two Guns placed in position at M.35.d.1.7. began firing at Gaps in wire 9.15 p.m. On receipt of notice that right post of Infantry was being swept from S.W. Guns decreased traverse to left 3 degrees and lifted 5 minutes. Guns were withdrawn at 3.15 AM.	
	4th		2 Guns replaced in Position in S edge of BOIS de RIAMONT. M.29.c.87.77 at 8.30 am in consequence of recapture of POWER STATION. Firing on wire was carried on with.	
	5th		Enemy Artillery active during day and night. Heavy T.Ms fell at intervals on CITE de RIAUMONT and CITE ST THEODORE. Large fire observed in LENS during night. The 2 Guns sent forward to positions on the S edge of BOIS de RIAMONT were withdrawn at 7.30 pm and took up their original positions.	
	6th		The 138th M.G. Coy relieved 7 of our Guns. No 1 Section, 4 Guns at M.18.a.95.35. No 4 Section in houses at M.17.c.68.68. (These 2 Section at present attached to 138th M.G. Coy) No 3 Section occupies Gun position 2s, 6 and 7. One Gun team at Coy H.Q. No 2 Section, position as before at 3s, 4s, 8 and 9. Enemy Artillery very active.	

P. Mahon
Major
Commdg 139 M.G. Coy

June 1917.

WAR DIARY or INTELLIGENCE SUMMARY
(Erase heading not required.)

Army Form C. 2118.

139th Machine Gun Company

Map Ref. 36 C. S.W. I

Place	Date	Hour	Summary of Events and Information	Remarks and references to Appendices
LIEVIN	7th		2/Lieut W. BLYTH rejoined from Rest Camp BOULOGNE. Enemy Artillery quiet during the night. Explosions were heard and fire seen in LENS. 6 Reinforcements arrived from Base Depot.	
	8th		Enemy Artillery active in afternoon against Batteries in M.28.a. At 8.20 pm enemy opened a Barrage on our front line, which lasted for about an hour, when he lifted on to a line CROOK – CRAZY, remaining on this line a considerable time. At about 8.55 pm a large fire was seen in the direction of the POWER STATION. At 8.33 pm in accordance with orders received from O.C. 138 M.G.Coy. eight of our guns opened fire. Three of these Guns acting in conjunction with our Artillery carried out a creeping Barrage. The other five Guns open fire on their fixed Barrage lines. All these Guns were firing continuously for 42 minutes and again at intervals until 3.30 am.	
	9th		Lieut W.H. HOFF rejoined from Course of Instruction. Enemy Artillery and M.G's less active than usual. At 11.10 pm the eight Guns attached to 138th M.G. Coy. were withdrawn in accordance with instructions from Bde. H.Q. 4 Guns returned to Coy H.Q. and 4 Guns to cellars at M.17.c.68.72.	
	10th		Company relieved by the 138th M.G. Company and proceeded to Rest billets at BULLY GRENAY.	
	12th		Lieut W.H. HOFF granted leave to U.K. 12/6/17 – 22/6/17.	
ST PIERRE	15th		Company relieved 137th M.G. Coy. in the Left Sector St PIERRE by 13 Guns in the line and 3 Guns in Reserve.	
	16th		Enemy Artillery active on our No 3 Gun with 77 m.m shells. Gas shells fell in front line and BUGS ALLEY during the night.	
	17th		2nd Canadians Bde. Pioneer Battn. dug and wired a new trench between CORKSCREW and COLLEGE trench.	A.J. Mahony Major Comdg 139. M.G. Coy

June 1917

WAR DIARY
or
INTELLIGENCE SUMMARY
(Erase heading not required.)

Army Form C. 2118.

139th Machine Gun Company

Map Ref. 36.C.S.W.I

Place	Date	Hour	Summary of Events and Information	Remarks and references to Appendices
ST PIERRE	17th		Enemy active during night shelling Cross Roads at M.11.d.65.80, also active with rifle grenades on COOPER TRENCH. Heavy T.Ms were fired at intervals around mouth of tunnel at M.1.C. central.	
	18th		Our Machine Guns kept wire open from Railway Embankment N.1.d.05.45 – N.7.b.10.99. Enemy Artillery shelled FOSSE 12 with 77mm shells at intervals during the night. 6 OR transferred to 16th M.G. Coy. 3 OR transferred to 18 M.G. Coy. } Under A.E's instructions. 8 OR transferred to 71st M.G. Coy.	
	19th		Enemy Artillery quieter than usual during night, but M.Gs very active.	
	20th		Enemy Artillery quiet during night. 2/Lieut H.L.C. GUTHRIE arrived from Base Depot and taken on strength.	
	19th		2/Lieut D.E.L. JONES } Transferred to 192nd M.G. Company 2/Lieut A.T. JONES }	
	23rd		Enemy T.Ms fired at intervals about CAVALRY TRENCH. 2/Lieut W.H. HOFF rejoined from leave to U.K.	
	24th		Enemy Machine Guns were active throughout the night sweeping roads in M.11.c and D, also CORKSCREW TRENCH. Enemy T.Ms were active against CITE ST THEODORE about 11.0 pm. About 20 4.2s fell in the vicinity of M.11.c.	
	25th		At 3.40 am enemy sent up several red lights, and then opened bombardment on the right; during the night he used a new type of star light, which, bursting at great height descended slowly, giving a very strong and brilliant light.	
	26th		Lieut C.D. POUND rejoined from Base Depot and taken on strength of Company. Enemy shelled houses in M.11.c and M.12.a at 6.30pm, 9.30pm and 11.45 pm little damage was done. CITE ST THEODORE and vicinity of FOSSE 9 reconnoitred during the night and again in the early morning for Gun positions north of FOSSE 9 found unsuitable. Positions finally chosen in CAVALRY TRENCH about M.18.d.1.4. Commdg. Railway Embankment in M.13.C.	

June. 1917.

WAR DIARY or INTELLIGENCE SUMMARY

(Erase heading not required.)

Army Form C. 2118.

139th Machine Gun Company

Map Ref. 36c. S.W. I

Place	Date	Hour	Summary of Events and Information	Remarks and references to Appendices
ST PIERRE.	27.		The 138 Infantry Brigade captured and consolidated objectives North of ACUE TRENCH. The 137 Infantry Brigade continued attack to the LENS - LIEVIN Road and ADROIT TRENCH and established posts therein. The 139 Infantry Brigade continued the consolidation of their line Northwards to FOSSE 9. The 139 M.G. Coy. Five Guns Barrage. Embankment and trenches from N.19.b.50.90. to N.19.b.80.40. These Guns from ZERO plus 15' onwards laid on their S.O.S. lines. Five Guns swept ALARM TRENCH from ZERO to ZERO plus 7'. All S.O.S Guns stood by for emergencies. after ZERO plus 15'. At the same time the Canadian Corps attacked on the Right of the Division. On the left the 6th Division Co-operated.	
	28.		Eight Machine Guns mounted in M.6.d. and laid on Barrage lines. Two Machine Guns held in readiness at M.18.d.06.32. Six Machine Guns in position to cover Brigade Front.	
	30.		8000 rounds fired on Barrage Lines. No retaliation. Enemy shelled CYCLIST TRENCH very heavily from 2.0 pm to 4.0 AM Tripods were buried and never completely knocked in about M.18.d.05.30. Enemy also intermittently shelled FOSSE 12 with T.M.S. Casualties during Month. 72068 Pte. ROGERS. E. ⎫ Wounded (Gas shell), but remained at Duty. (3/6/17). 67889 Pte STOCKDALE G. ⎭ 12460 Pte. DILKS. F.S. Wounded (Gas shell) 17/6/17. 35304 Pte SPEDDING E. Wounded (Gas shell) 17/6/17. 86436 Pte. FARRAR D. Wounded (shrapnel) 26/6/17. 72093 Cpl. BURTON F. Slightly wounded 27/6/17 and remained at Duty.	

H. D. Watson
Major
Commdg 139th M.G. Coy.

June 1917.

WAR DIARY
or
INTELLIGENCE SUMMARY
(Erase heading not required.)

139th Machine Gun Coy

Army Form C. 2118.

Map Ref. 36.C S.W. I

Place	Date	Hour	Summary of Events and Information	Remarks and references to Appendices

ST PIERRE			Approximate number of rounds expended during month. 172,350 rounds. This includes 11800 rounds fired by A.A. Guns.
			Work Done. LIEVIN TRENCHES
			Cleaning out Dug-outs and cellars.
			Improving and strengthening Gun Positions. Deepening trench to No 7. Gun.
			Building emplacement at No 2 Gun at house M.23.70.00.
			Deepening trench at No 9 Gun and improving emplacement.
			4 Position dug in CRIMSON TRENCH M.17.b and M.17.d.
			Emplacement dug and completed for 4 Guns at M.18.a.05.33 B.4 Group.
			Emplacements dug and completed for 4 Guns at M.17.d.68.68 B.3 Group.
			Constructing A.A. Mounting at M.18.a.80.50
			Belt filling and carrying S.A.A.
			    ST PIERRE TRENCHES.
			Cleaning out Dug-outs and cellars.
			Improving dug-out and emplacement at No 6 Position (M.6.a.40.72.)
			Emplacements completed at M.12.a.68.70 and M.11.c.90.96.
			Latrines dug in MUSIC TRENCH.
			Emplacements completed at M.11.b.81., M.12.a.54.76., M.11.a.66.48., M.11.d.45.12.
			Shell slit made at No 3 Position. M.6.25.50.
			Belt filling and carrying S.A.A.
			Programme of Training while in Rest Billets.
			C.O Inspection each morning. Physical Training and handling of arms. Indication and Recognition of targets, Advance Gun Drill. Gas Helmet Drill. Route March.
			                                                          L.J Mahon Major
			                                                Commdg 139th M.G. Coy	

July 1917

WAR DIARY
or
INTELLIGENCE SUMMARY
(Erase heading not required.)

Army Form C.2118.

Vol 18

139th Machine Gun Company

Place	Date	Hour	Summary of Events and Information	Remarks and references to Appendices
ST PIERRE	1st		Company in trenches at ST PIERRE. Tunnel at M.18.d.1.4 heavily shelled most of the day. FOSSE 12 near COSSACK Gun Position bombarded with Trench Mortars.	Map ref.— 36 C SW 1
"	3rd		Special Barrage put across N.13.d from N. to S. to arrest threatened enemy counter attack. Company relieved by the 6th Canadian M.G. Coy and enbussed at BULLY GRENAY for FREVILLERS	
FREVILLERS	4th		Company arrived at Billets FREVILLERS 6-30AM.	
"	2nd		Lieut M.A. HART granted Leave to U.K.	
"	6th		C.S.M. NASH J. transferred from 101st M.G. Coy and taken on strength of Coy.	
"	7th		Demonstration of M.G. Fire at MARQUEFFLES FARM	
"	8th		2 Lieut H.W. BROWN proceeded on Course of Instruction at Corps Central School	
"			Brigade Church Parade at Training Area near HERLIN.	
"	12th		Lieut R.J.C. SHIPLEY admitted to Hospital sick, and evacuated to No. 22. C.C.S.	
"	13th		Inspection of Transport by G.O.C. MAGNICOURT – CHELERS Rd.	
"	14th		Lieut M.A HART rejoined from Leave.	
"			5 O.R. transferred from 192 M.G. Coy and taken on strength of Coy.	
"	15		2 Lieut H.W. BROWN rejoined from Course of Instruction	
"	16th		G.O.C inspected Sections in Immediate Action by day & night Judging Distances, Indication and Recognition of Targets, Combined Drill & M.G. Signals, Action from Packs and Changing position forward	
"			Lieut R.J.C SHIPLEY discharged Hospital	
"	17th		Lieut R.J.C SHIPLEY proceeded on short leave to U.K.	
"			Inspection by G.O.C on Ground P.32.a.05.	
"	18th		10 O.R reinforcements arrived from Base Depot and taken on strength of Coy.	R.Raff Lieut /c 139 M.G.C

July 1917

WAR DIARY or INTELLIGENCE SUMMARY

(Erase heading not required.)

Army Form C. 2118.

139th Machine Gun Company

Place	Date	Hour	Summary of Events and Information	Remarks and references to Appendices
FREVILLERS	23rd		Company moved into new billets at FOUQUIERES.	
	24th		Lieut E.C. HOLDEN proceeded on short leave to U.K.	
VERMELLES	25th		Company relieved the 71st M.G. Coy in the trenches at VERMELLES	
	26th		St GEORGES POST GUN had to be taken into dug-out for an hour and a half during the night owing to Hostile T.M. fire.	
	27th		Suspected enemy O.P. in SLAG HEAP G.5.a.72	
	27th		Lieut W.H.B. REZIN proceeded on short leave to U.K.	
	28th		Hostile Trench Mortar fire very lively round St GEORGES trench during the day necessitating the dismounting of Anti-Aircraft Gun for a time.	
			Major H.D. MATSON and 2.O.R. proceeded to CAMIERS on Course of Instruction.	
	30th		At 8.45 P.M. enemy put 18. 5.9 shells into LA ROTOIRE at G.15.b. and D	
			Lieut. R.J.C. SHIPLEY rejoined from leave to U.K.	

Programme of Training while in Rest Billets

Physical Training, Immediate Action by day and night, Judging Distances, Indication and Recognition of targets, Combined Drill and M.G. Signals, Open Warfare section on a Flank advancing. and Tactical Exercises.

Casualties.
72089 Pte BENTLEY H. wound of arm 1/7/17.
88164 " BROWN F.C. wound of head 1/7/17 (remains at Duty).
37426 " WILLIAMS E. shrapnel wound of leg 31/7/17
28205 " BENNETT C. wounded Gas shell 31/7/17

Approx number of rounds fired during month = 71.200 rounds.

R.P.S.P.
Lieut.
O.C. 139th M.G.Coy

WAR DIARY or INTELLIGENCE SUMMARY

August 1917

139th Machine Gun Company

Army Form C. 2118.

Vol 19

Place	Date	Hour	Summary of Events and Information	Remarks and references to Appendices
VERMELLES	1st		Company in Trenches at VERMELLES. At 11.0 pm several gas shells were sent over in the vicinity of C.12.c.3.4. From 2 am to 2.50 am DUDLEY DUMP was bombarded with heavy Trench Mortars. 3. O.R. Reinforcements arrived from Base Depot and taken on strength of Company.	
	2nd		GORDON ALLEY and O.B.1. were shelled with 4.2s and gas shells at intervals during day & evening.	
	3rd		On RIGHT Sub-section, enemy S O S signal at midnight brought down enemy Barrage, and all our positions were shelled. The emplacement at DEVON DUMP was destroyed. Barrage ceased at 12.30 am and the rest of the night was quiet. Lieut. M. BLYTH proceeded on short leave to U.K.	
	4th		A Raid was delivered by the 8th Battn. Sherwood Foresters. The M.G. Team of the Coy. went over to the first halt with R.E. party and Lewis Gun Teams. When the Barrage lifted, the team ran forward and took up a position in a shell hole on the left flank, about 35 to 40 yards to left of tape. The enemy was firing rapid rifle fire from the LEFT flank, also a M.G. which fired high. The enemy barrage was put down on our front line and well behind the Gun team. It was fairly strong and consisted of T.Ms. of all calibres. The enemy to the left front of the team were throwing grenades in large quantities, and firing rifles. The Gun was placed in action but did not fire. The Infantry had pushed forward, and one of the team who had become separated had gone forward with a Lewis Gun team, reaching the enemy's barbed wire. At that moment the whistle to retire was blown, and all troops of the left party came back, with the exception of the M.G. Team, who had not heard the whistle or seen the parties retiring. By chance, however, the Corporal i/c happened to stand up to look round for any possible target, when he saw the RIGHT party coming back, whereupon he ordered the team to retire. All the Gun Positions were heavily shelled between 11.30 pm and 12.30 am, in some cases necessitating the dismounting of the Gun. Lieut. E.G. HOLDEN rejoined from short leave to U.K.	R.K off Lieut D.C.
	7th		The positions in Close Support on the RIGHT Sector were shelled with gas from Trench Mortars between 12.30 am and 2.30 am. Lieut. W.H.B. REED rejoined from leave to U.K.	

August 1917.

WAR DIARY
or
INTELLIGENCE SUMMARY
(Erase heading not required.)

Army Form C. 2118.

139th Machine Gun Company

Place	Date	Hour	Summary of Events and Information	Remarks and references to Appendices
VERMELLES	8th		Lieut H.L.C. GUTHRIE admitted to Hospital (sick).	
	9th		The Gun at DEVON DUMP was hit by shrapnel, piercing the barrel casing, and rendering the Gun unserviceable. Lieut H.N. BROWN proceeded on short leave to U.K.	
	10th		Enemy artillery was very active shelling CHAPEL ALLEY. Lieut R.J.C. SHIPLEY slightly wounded in face, but remained at Duty.	
	11th		Enemy put down heavy barrage on LEFT Sub-Sector at 9.30 pm. DEVON LANE and CHAPEL ALLEY were heavily shelled. Entrance to R 51 dug-out was blown in.	
	12th		GORDON ALLEY and O.B.1 were shelled with about 100 rounds of Trench Mortars.	
	13/14		A combined Operation was carried out by the 5th and 6th Battns. Sherwood Foresters against the enemy Front and Support lines near the HULLUCH Road. The 139th M.G.Coy in co-operation with the 137th M.G.Coy put up a Box Barrage. 2 O.R. Reinforcements arrived from Base Depot and taken on Strength of Company.	
	16th		The 139th Machine Gun Company was relieved by the 138th Machine Gun Company and proceeded to Rest Billets at FOUQUIERES. Lieut H. BLYTH rejoined from leave to U.K.	
FOUQUIERES	18th		Lieut C.D POUND proceeded on short leave to U.K.	
	20th		Company moved to new Billets at DROUVIN.	
DROUVIN	22nd		Lieut H.N. BROWN rejoined from short leave to U.K.	R.Poll
	24th		Sports held in conjunction with 8th Battn. Sherwood Foresters. Major H.D. MATSON and 2 ORs rejoined from Course of Instruction at CAMIERS. Major H.D. MATSON proceeded on short leave to U.K.	Lieut Fl. Oy M.G.C
	25th		Company relieved the 99th M.G.Coy in the CAMBRIN Sector. Coy H.Qrs.- ANNEQUIN FOSSE. Dispositions. 2 Sections in the Line, 1 Section in Reserve, 1 Section in Rest Billets FOUQUIERES. Transport Lines SAILLY.	

August 1917

WAR DIARY or INTELLIGENCE SUMMARY

(Erase heading not required.)

Army Form C. 2118.

139th Machine Gun Company

Place	Date	Hour	Summary of Events and Information	Remarks and references to Appendices
ANNEQUIN	27th		2 OR Reinforcements arrived from Base Depot and taken on Strength of Company.	
	30th		1 OR Reinforcement arrived from Base Depot and taken on Strength of Company.	

Programme of Training while in Rest Billets

Physical Training, Immediate Action, Indication and Recognition of Targets, Judging Distances, Firing on Range, Swimming.

Work Done VERMELLES

Repairing trenches, New emplacement at G.11.c.69.22. for daylight firing.
Rebuilding of covered emplacement at R.51.

Work Done CAMBRIN Sector.

Repairs to Trenches and Gun Positions.
Cookhouse constructed near R.58., Dug-out renovated at R.63.

Casualties during month:—

102403 Pte HOWELLS. J.O. Accidentally Wounded 3/8/17
81306 Pte FIRTH.A. Wounded, shrapnel of head and shoulders 4/8/17
45035 Pte MITTON. A. ⎫
72084 Pte FLISHER H. ⎬ Wounded (Gas Shell) 8/8/17
24208 Sgt. SMITH.J.F. ⎭
Lieut R.J.C. SHIPLEY slight wound of face, but remained at Duty. 10/8/17
99258 Pte. BROWN.A. Shell wound of neck and arm 11/8/17

Approx. number of rounds expended during month = 273,250 rounds.

R. Lov. Lieut
OC 139th M.G. Coy.

September 1917

WAR DIARY
or
INTELLIGENCE SUMMARY.
(Erase heading not required.)

Army Form C. 2118.

139th Machine Gun Company

Vol 20

Place	Date	Hour	Summary of Events and Information	Remarks and references to Appendices
CAMBRIN SECTOR. ANNEQUIN	1		Map Ref. 36. N.W. 1/20,000 Company in Trenches. CAMBRIN SECTOR. H.Q. ANNEQUIN. Two Gun Positions at R.57 & V.39 taken over by 176th M.G. Coy. in accordance with Divisional orders. Arrangements completed for taking over Gun Position at A.27.3 held by 5th M.G. Coy (2nd Division). Enemy attempted raid on our trenches at 4.45 A.M. Heavy barrage fell on "Old Boots" trench. A shell bursting on parados at R.59 destroyed the spare parts case and blew team to the bottom of the dug-out.	Disposition of Guns Attached
	4th		Arrangements completed for sniping with M.Gs. Position at R.66 connected by telephone to "BOBBY" O.P. Parties of Germans using track immediately west of HAISNES Church, caught by our fire and scattered.	
	5th		Gas was projected into OLD BOOTS trench near R.63, and to the right of it. The effects was felt in ANNEQUIN.	
	6th		At 11.45 P.M. train heard behind enemy lines near AUCHY. Cheering was heard on its arrival there.	
	7th		Lieut. E.B. WOODFORDE granted special leave to U.K. (one month). 8 O.Rs. reinforcements taken on strength from Base Depot.	
	8th		Major H.D. MATSON, rejoined from leave to U.K.	
	10th		Lieut H.L.C. GUTHRIE rejoined from Rest Camp. Lieut R. PAGE granted leave to U.K. from 10.9.17 - 24.9.17.	
	11/12th		8th Battn. Sherwood Foresters raided with 3 Offrs and 90 O.Rs. the enemy trenches within the points - A.28.c.41.71., A.28.c.41.78., A.28.c.03.99 and A.28.c.24.91.	Eric G. Hooder Lt
	12th		Red light reported signalling 9.30 P.M. to 9.45 P.M. Flashing reported answering :- at each pause, white light, direction of CAMBRIN.	
	13th		Signalling again observed between CAMBRIN and AUCHY.	

September 1917

WAR DIARY or INTELLIGENCE SUMMARY.

139th Machine Gun Company

Army Form C. 2118.

Place	Date	Hour	Summary of Events and Information	Remarks and references to Appendices
ANNEQUIN. CAMBRIN SECTOR.	15		9. ORs reinforcements arrived at 46th Divisional Depot Battn. and taken on strength of Company.	
	17		2/Lieut: E.H. BENNETT, arrived from Base Depot and taken on strength of Coy.	Disposition of Guns attached
SAILLY LABOURSE	19		Company relieved on the afternoon of the 19th inst by the 99th M.G. Coy. and marched to billets at SAILLY LABOURSE, Reserve section remaining in billets at FOUQUIERES.	
			Map Ref. LOOS 1/10,000. LENS 1/10,000	
	23rd		Company relieved four Guns of the 71st M.G. Coy and established a 4 Gun Battery in a position in LOOS Trench, and also relieved 6 Guns of the 18th M.G. Coy.	
			Advanced HQRS. TRIANGLE POST	
			REAR HQRS. MAZINGARBE POST. Office.	
MAZINGARBE. 14.DIS. SECTOR.	24		Gas shells fell from 10.15 pm regularly until morning between RESERVE Trench and PETIT LOOS. Enemy fired H.T.M. bombs intermittently throughout the night at HORSE ALLEY.	
	25		Lieut: R PAGE, rejoined from leave to U.K.	
	26		At 10.0 pm and throughout the night gas shells fell between LOOS and RAILWAY ALLEY.	
	27		2. OR reinforcements arrived from No 1 A.S.C. Section A.H.T Depot and taken on strength.	
	30		2/Lieut: E H BENNETT transferred to the 137 Machine Gun Company.	
	29		At 4.30 a.m. enemy opened heavy T.M bombardment consisting of H.T.M's and Wing-bombs on H.25.d, under cover of which a small hostile raiding party penetrated our lines, at about H.25.d.40.65. The Machine Gunners at H.26.c 28 40 caught sight of this party working its way along HORSE ALLEY. It consisted of 1 Offr., 1 N.C.O. and four men. It was promptly bombed by our Machine Gunners, and made off in the direction of the position at H.32.a.25.80. When the party was passing the dug-out near H.26.c/20.40 one of our men emerged from it and was fired at by the German Offr. with a revolver, but was missed. The party then disappeared. During the bombardment one dug-out suffered a direct hit, and 2 boxes of S.A.A. were fired.	E.G. Horsley Lt

September 1917

WAR DIARY or INTELLIGENCE SUMMARY.

Army Form C. 2118.

139th Machine Gun Coy.

Place	Date	Hour	Summary of Events and Information	Remarks and references to Appendices
MAZINGARBE 14 BIS SECTOR			Map Ref. LOOS 1/10,000. LENS 1/10,000. <u>Work Done</u>. CAMBRIN SECTOR. Rebuilt emplacement at R.60. Four new emplacements (open) built for Battery at V.48. Rebuilt emplacement at R.66 and Parados at R.62. Improving emplacements at V.48. Revetment of Trench by R.64. Anti-Aircraft mounting placed in position at A.27.d.27.34. <u>Work Done</u>. 14.BIS. 3 Battle Emplacements completed. Emplacements revetted. Anti-Aircraft mounting fixed. <u>Casualties during month</u>. 43678 Cpl MATKIN L.A. Killed in Action 14.9.17. Approx. number of rounds expended during month = 176,100 rounds. Anti-Aircraft fired approx. 4,040 rounds.	Disposition of Guns attached Eric G. Holden

139th Machine Gun Company
6.9.17.

DISPOSITIONS

CAMBRIN SECTOR.

From Left to Right.

LEFT SUB-SECTOR.

Section Headquarters :- MAISON ROUGE. A.26.b.48.40.

A.27.3. -------------------A.27.a.75.23.
R. 66. -------------------A. 27.c.90.98.
R. 65. -------------------A.27.c.95.80. (A.A.).
R. 64. -------------------A.27.d.25.40.

RIGHT SUB-SECTOR.

Section Headquarters :- BARTS ALLEY. G. 4.c.57.03.

R. 63. -------------------G.3.b.65.90.
R. 60. -------------------G.4.a.11.40.
R. 59. -------------------G.4.a.17.10.
R. 58. -------------------G.4.c.40.25. (A.A.).

VILLAGE LINE.

V. 45. -------------------A.26.d.25.75. (A.A.).
V. 44. -------------------A.26.d.33.60.

TWO GUNS IN RESERVE AT COMPANY HEADQUARTERS, ANNEQUIN, FOSSE, L.5.b.65.85.

139th Machine Gun Company   24.9.17.

DISPOSITIONS.

14 BIS. SECTOR.

LEFT SUB-SECTOR.

BOIS HUGO 1 ------------------------------ H.25.d.85.36.
BOIS HUGO 2. ----------------------------- H.26.c.15.40.
HULL ALLEY ------------------------------- H.25.d.75.12.
HUMBUG ALLEY ----------------------------- H.32.a.20.85.

RIGHT SUB-SECTOR.

No.7 ------------------------------------- H.32.a.26.26.
No.6 ------------------------------------- H.32.a.25.21.
No.5. ------------------------------------ H.32.c.10.78.
No.4 ------------------------------------- H.32.c.08.65.
No.3 ------------------------------------- H.32.c.01.60.
No.2 ------------------------------------- H.32.c.98.50.

Four Gun Battery Position at G.36.b.74.65.

Anti-Aircraft ---------------------------- G.36.b.74.65.

139th Machine Gun Company

DISPOSITION OF GUNS

26.8.17.

CAMBRIN SECTOR.

From Left to Right.

V. 48 ------------------- A. 26.b.65.35.   (Anti-Aircraft).
V. 45 ------------------- A. 26.d.25.75.   (Anti-Aircraft).
R. 66 ------------------- A. 27.c.90.98.
R. 65 ------------------- A. 27.c.95.80.
R. 64 ------------------- A. 27.d.25.40.
R. 63 ------------------- G. 3.b.65.90.
R. 62 ------------------- G. 3.b.80.88.
R. 60 ------------------- G. 4.a.11.40.
R. 59 ------------------- G. 4.a.17.10.
R. 58 ------------------- G. 4.c.40.25.
R. 57 ------------------- G. 4.c.50.12.
V. 39 ------------------- G. 9.a.80.82.   (Anti-Aircraft).

October 1917

WAR DIARY

PAGE I

139th Machine Gun Company

Vol 21

Place	Date	Hour	Summary of Events and Information	Remarks and references to Appendices
MAZINGARBE	1st		9 O.R. Reinforcements arrived at 46th Divisional Depot Batt. and taken on strength of Company	
	2nd		1 O.R. No 31681 Rejoined from Leave to U.K.	
	3rd		1 O.R. No 37428 Rejoined from Leave to U.K.	
	4th		Major Matson proceeded to Boulogne, for America and struck of Strength of Company. (Authority - 46th Divisional wire A/938 dated 3-10-17)	
	7th		2 O.R. No- 24217 - No 24259 Granted leave to U.K.	
	8th		Lieut. E.B. Woodford Rejoined from Leave to U.K.	

October

WAR DIARY or INTELLIGENCE SUMMARY.

Page II   Army Form C. 2118.

139 M G Company

Place	Date	Hour	Summary of Events and Information	Remarks and references to Appendices

REF LOOS 36c NW 3'/10000

MAZINGARBE | 8th | | Antiaircraft position shelled for about 15 minutes with 4.2 after firing at E.A. No damage was done. Harassing fire 1500 rounds. A-A fire 250 rounds. | |
	9th		Harassing fire 1000 rounds.	
	10th		" " 750 rounds. Gun at HELL strong point withdrawn to junction of O.G.1 + new Support Tr.	
	11th		" " 1750 rounds. A A fire 1000 rounds.	I.O.R. No. 33533 Returned from leave to U.K
	12th	10.30am	1 " " with direct hit on No 7 position (HEAVEN TRENCH).	
		4.30pm	E A flying low over trenches engaged with rifle fire, + retaliated with M G fire. During night enemy M G's fired on LOOS TR. Harassing fire 3000 rounds. A-A fire 1000 rounds.	
	13th		" " 1500 "	
	14th		Between 8 am + 10 am E A were very active over Hill 70. Harassing fire 1500 rounds. A A fire 1000 rounds.	I.O.R. No. 74269 Granted Leave U.K
	15th		One gun team withdrawn from HEAVEN to Battery. E.A. flying high, were active over Hill 70. Enemy M G's fired on LOOS TR during night. Harassing fire 1750 rounds.	Lieut Guthrie H.S.C. Granted leave to U.K
	16th		Enemy fired salvos of 77 mm on HURDLE TR all day. Harassing fire 1750 rounds. A A fire 1500 rounds	

J.M.Webster
Capt.

October — Page III — Army Form C. 2118.

WAR DIARY or INTELLIGENCE SUMMARY

139 M G Company

Place	Date	Hour	Summary of Events and Information	Remarks and references to Appendices
MAZINGARBE	17th		Harassing fire 2000 rounds. AA fire 500 rounds. One gun withdrawn from HURDLE O Battery.	
	18th	8.45 pm	Intense bombardment of Left Subsector. Gun at HULL Strong point destroyed & the two sentries killed. Harassing fire 3000 rounds. 2 OR. No 24259 No 24217 Returned from leave to UK	
	19th		Harassing fire 2750 rounds. AA fire 500 rounds.	
	20th		" " 3000 rounds.	
	21st	5 pm 8.7 pm	H 25 d & H 26 c shelled, a direct hit being obtained on gun in HUMBUG. E.A. fighting patrol active during morning, but remained out of M G range. Harassing fire 3000 rounds. 2. OR. No 7586 – No 4452 Granted leave to UK	
	22nd	10.45 pm	12 4.2 shells fell just short of 'O' Battery LOOS T.R. Harassing fire 3000 rounds.	
	23rd	5.30 pm	Considerable movement again reported between BOIS DE QUATORZE & BOIS DE DIXHUIT. Spasmodic shelling of Left Subsector, occasionally increasing to considerable intensity. HURDLE & R shelled with 77 mm & 105 mm. Harassing fire 3000 rounds. 2 OR. No 24230 – No 27099 Left for course in UK and struck off strength of Company	
	24th		Harassing fire 3750. AA fire 750	O W Blakben Capt

October — WAR DIARY or INTELLIGENCE SUMMARY — Page IIII — Army Form C. 2118 — 139 M.G. Company

Place	Date	Hour	Summary of Events and Information	Remarks and references to Appendices
MAZINGARBE	25th	3.30pm	HTM shell fell in trench at H.25.d.45.4, opening old mine tunnel. This was followed for a considerable distance towards enemy lines, & its existence reported to Brigade & OC Supp Battalion. 10R N. 20269 Rejoined from leave to UK. Harassing fire 3000 rounds.	
	26th		" " 3000 "	
	27th		" " 3000 "	
	28th		In consequence of enemy movement over the top South of BOIS DE QUATORZE, a sniping MG has been stationed in HURDLE TR. Observer uses Artillery O.P. Harassing fire 3500 rounds.	
	29th		Lieut Guthrie HLC Rejoined from leave to UK. Successful fire projection. During enemy retaliation, 3 direct hits were obtained on HUMBUG near gun position. New Divisional Barrage Scheme brought in to use. Harassing fire 1250, AA fire 500	
	30th		1 77 mm direct hit obtained on HURDLE by sniping gun. Harassing fire 3 & 500 rounds. AA fire 600 rounds	
	31st		" " 1000 rounds " 650	
	29		2 OR. N. 24233 – N. 37229 Granted leave to UK.	

October

WAR DIARY
or
INTELLIGENCE SUMMARY.

Page IV   Army Form C. 2118.

139 M.G. Company

Place	Date	Hour	Summary of Events and Information	Remarks and references to Appendices

Summary

Casualties

No 99394 Pte H. Freeman — Killed in action 19.11.17
No 85917 Pte G. Yare — Killed in action 17.11.17

Rounds fired (approximate)
Harassing fire   56,250
Anti-Aircraft fire   8,250
                    ———
Total   64,500

Work done

9 Battle Emplacements built or rebuilt.
12 Emplacements built for operations.
LOOS TRENCH boarded.
HURDLE TR (part of) boarded.
Latrines Cook house built, two dug-outs recovered & cleared.

November 1917.   **WAR DIARY**   Page 1.   Army Form C. 2118.
                                        or
Instructions regarding War Diaries and Intelligence   **INTELLIGENCE SUMMARY.**   139th Machine Gun Company
Summaries are contained in F. S. Regs., Part II.
and the Staff Manual respectively. Title pages   (Erase heading not required.)
will be prepared in manuscript.

Place	Date	Hour	REF. LOOS 36cNW 1/10.000. Summary of Events and Information	Remarks and references to Appendices

MAZINGARBE

1st — New Positions built in HURDLE TRENCH. Repairs to trench and emplacements at LOOS TRENCH. 25.500 Rounds were fired during raid.

2. — The trench in immediate proximity to No 10 Position (BOIS HUGO) was blown in at 3 pm. by a number of light T.M. bombs. Harassing fire 2000 rds.

3. — Enemy retaliated yesterday on HURDLE TRENCH between 3.30 & 4 pm. Harassing fire 5000 rds. — Work putting A. frames in LOOS TRENCH.

4. — Deepening trench at HUMBUG & HELL POST. Harassing fire 2000 rds. Lieut W.H. Stoff Granted leave to UK 4.11.17 to 18.11.17

5. — On the night of 4th/5th Nov. the 1/6th S. Foresters raided the enemy at H.32.d. The programme of firing was carried out without alteration until 9.5 pm when a succession of red lights was observed on the exact bearing of our S.O.S. lines, and at the same time heavy firing was heard in that direction (HILL 70 LEFT). Before 4 lights had gone up. 3 guns had switched from the raid Target on to their normal S.O.S. lines and continued firing until the bombardment appeared to die down. The other 3 guns were maintained on their raid barrage, and it afterwards turned out that the red lights were an enemy signal. — During & after the raid it was found impossible to keep the guns in HUMBUG and HEAVEN mounted owing to continual shelling by

WAR DIARY or INTELLIGENCE SUMMARY.

Page II.

Army Form C. 2118.

139º Machine Gun Company

Place	Date	Hour	Summary of Events and Information	Remarks and references to Appendices
MAZINGARBE	5.		Meda Trench mortar Bombs. The 3 guns in HURDLE fired throughout the raid in spite of the enemy's artillery barrage which fell just in front of HURDLE. 23.000 rounds were fired Raid & S.O.S. Barrages. 2/Lt Blyth W. received small shrapnel wound in arm in HEAVEN TRENCH during the raid.	
	6.		Harassing fire 2.500 rounds. Building alternative Battery positions	
	7.		Harassing fire 2.500 rounds. 6. alternative battery positions completed at G.36.b.85.64. to G.36.b.94.54. Waterproof shelters erected for use of guns during day time.	
	8.		Harassing fire 3.000 rds. Repairing Sap between dugout & emplacement in HEAVEN, which was blown in on previous night	
	9.		Harassing fire 3.500 rounds. 97 boxes S.A.A. carried up to Battery. Deepening Trenches at the Battery. Lieut M.A. Hart transferred to Base Depôt being supernumerary to Establishment	
	10".		At 8.10 pm enemy put up 4 Red lights in succession. At 12.10 am put up 2 Green lights. At 12.40 put up 2 Red lights. No action appeared to follow on any occasion. Harassing fire 3.000 rounds.	

WAR DIARY or INTELLIGENCE SUMMARY.

Page III.

Army Form C. 2118.

139th Machine Gun Company

Place	Date	Hour	Summary of Events and Information	Remarks and references to Appendices
MAZINGARBE	11th		3.30 – 4.30 pm. Heavy shelling from HULLUCH to CITE ST AUGUSTE with 5.9" & 4.2" H.T.Ms. Harassing fire 3000 rounds. A.A. 500.	
	12th		LOOS TRENCH was shelled at 9 am with H.V. 4.2". Harassing fire 2.500rds	
	13th		Harassing fire 2.500 rounds. Work:- Clearing trenches, building new emplacements. Clearing dug-out entrance, blown in by shell fire.	
	14th		Harassing fire 3000 rounds	
	15th		Harassing fire 3000 rounds.	
	16th		Harassing fire 3.000 rounds. A.A. 250 rounds. Clearing obstructions in field of fire of gun in O.G.2. Lieut Blyth rejoined from evacuation & taken on strength. "D" Battery LOOS TRENCH taken over by 1 section of 138th M.G. Coy at 11.15 pm. After relief, proceeded to the New Right sub-Sector.	R.50, R.51 DUDLEY, DEVON
VERMELLES	17th		139th Coy. relieved the 138th Coy at VERMELLES BREWERY (H.2) Two Sections taking over the new Left sub-Sector & (Battery R.52, R.53, R.54, R.55) (5 guns & 1 AA at H.2³.)	
	18th		The remaining Section in the old (H4) Sector, was relieved at 10.30 am & marched to billets at Sailly Labourse. Relief completed.	
	19th		Harassing fire 1750 rounds — E.A. flew low over front line at 10.30 am. Gas shells fell between O.B.1 & HULLUCH ROAD at 10.45 pm. Revetment of trenches at Battery, Repairs to Camouflage at R.54. Lieut W.H. Hoy rejoined from UK	

WAR DIARY or INTELLIGENCE SUMMARY.
(Erase heading not required.)

Page IV.　　Army Form C. 2118.

139º Machine Gun Company

Place	Date	Hour	Summary of Events and Information	Remarks and references to Appendices
VERMELLES	20.		At 9.30 pm Enemy opened fire with 5.9ˢ H.T.M.S. & winged bombs. 5.9ˢ fell in DEVON LANE. H.T.Mˢ & winged bombs fell in near vicinity of DUDLEY DUMP. One falling 10ʸ from Tripod. at 10pm. blowing part of emplacement in. Harassing fire 2500ʳᵈˢ	
	21.		In response to S.O.S. Sent up on HILL 70 front. 4.500 rounds were fired. Work:- Preparing trench between N. 1 Position Right Sector & A.A. position & returfing all positions in Right Sector.	
	22.		About 7 AM E.A. was observed flying over front line so low that gun could not be depressed sufficiently to fire. Harassing fire 4.500 rounds.	
	23.		2 O.R. Reinforcements arrived at 46ᵗʰ Div. Training Battⁿ & taken on Strength. At 10.30. Enemy fired abt 20 H.V. Shells. falling short, & just over Battery. Several winged bombs fell round DOOLEY POST.	
	24.		Two men were observed digging trench on top of DUMP. C.S. a 92 at 7.30 am They only appeared occasionally. Observers reported movement to be NIL yesterday. At 7 AM. a party of 50 !! of the enemy were seen moving in front of HAISNES It was impossible to register sniping gun correctly owing to gusty wind. 1. O.R. Wounded Harassing fire. 4.500 rounds A.A. 750 Rounds.	
	25.		M.G. firing over DEVON LANE Active during night. Harassing 4.500 rounds	
	26.		Harassing fire. 4500 Rounds. Work:- Revetting & boarding trenches	

WAR DIARY or INTELLIGENCE SUMMARY

Page V. — Army Form C. 2118.

139th Machine Gun Company

Place	Date	Hour	Summary of Events and Information	Remarks and references to Appendices
VERMELLES	27		Harassing fire. 3000 Rounds. Work :- Strengthening position at R.55. Parapet at OOZLEY slightly lowered to allow gun to traverse.	
	28		Harassing fire. 3.600 Rounds. Work. Deepening trench at R.54. Occupation of new position at FREUND DUMP giving up R.51. 1. OR. Wounded.	
	29		4.2" & 5.9s bombardments at 5.45 & 11.35 pm on HULLUCH ROAD & CHAPEL ALLEY. Harassing fire 5.500 Rounds. Work :- I Frames put in V. BATTERY.	
	30		Considerable activity of enemy Trench mortars during night near DEVON DUMP. Emplacement at R.51 slightly damaged by 5-9s Activity at R.53 & R.52 throughout night. 3 OR Reinforcements arrived at 46th Div. I. Base & taken on Strength of Coy.	

Work Done at 14 B.I.S SECTOR
Rebuilt 4 Positions in HURDLE TRENCH.
Built 6 Alternative Positions at BATTERY
Deepening trenches at HUMBUG, HELL POST, T. BATTERY.

Work Done at VERMELLES SECTOR
Built Position at FREUND DUMP
Parapit at OOZLEY slightly lowered to allow gun to traverse.
Revetment of trenches at BATTERY

Casualties during month.
Lieut Blyth & 3 ORs. Wounded.

Approx. number of rounds fired during month

129.750 Tr.
1.600. A.A. 10.
131.350 Total.

December, 1917.

WAR DIARY or INTELLIGENCE SUMMARY. 139th Machine Gun Company

Page I.   Army Form C. 2118.

VR 23

Place	Date	Hour	REF. LOOS. 36 C N.W. 1/10.000 Summary of Events and Information	Remarks and references to Appendices
VERMELLES	1st		At 7.30 pm DEVON LANE and entrance to shaft were blown in and M.G. emplacement wrecked. At 2.45 p.m. 7.30 pm + 12.30 am enemy trench mortared very heavily round R.55. + R.54 + R.56. At 12.30 am R.55 + R.56 were obliterated. Also R.52 shelled at 7.45 am + 12.45 am at least 5 direct hits into trench. In response to S.O.S. on left division front at 7.30 p.m. 11.950 Rds were fired. In response to S.O.S. on left division front at 12.30 a.m. 10.250 Rds were fired. Harassing fire 1500 Rds.	
	2.		At 4 pm enemy fired 3. 5.9s H. Shell which filled in trench about 20 yds from R.55. Position. 1 O.R. Killed in Action. Harassing fire. 1750 Rds.	
	3.		Slight enemy activity with H.T.Ms between 11.pm and midnight. Harassing fire. 3.600	
	4.		Harassing fire. 4.500 A.A. Gun 500 Rds.	
	5.		Heavy shelling of O.B.I. 8 pm – 8.30 pm. Between 2.30 + 3.30 pm. 6.30 + 7.30 pm enemy bombarded G.12 c + d. with H.T.Ms M.T.M. 5.9s + 4.2s. One red light was observed about 6 pm but no further developments. Harassing fire. 3.900 Rds	
	6.		Between 2.30 + 4.30 pm enemy bombarded the area G.12.c + d with H.T.Ms. 5.9s + 4.2s and again 11.45 pm L.T. M's fell in front of St GEORGE'S POST. An enemy M.G. was playing low round R.51 all through the night. Between 7. + 8. Am E.A. were active over the area H.12 c + d flying in the direction of VERMELLES. Harassing fire. 6.250 Rds.	

December 1917. WAR DIARY or INTELLIGENCE SUMMARY. Page II. 139th Machine Gun Company. Army Form C. 2118.

Place	Date	Hour	Summary of Events and Information	Remarks and references to Appendices
VERMELLES	7		Between 3.30 & 4.30 pm enemy bombarded area H.12.c & d. This occurred again at midnight & intermittently during this morning. Twice yesterday enemy dropped a H.T.M. in front of FREUND DUMP each time the dug-out entrance & emplacement had to be repaired. About 2 am 3 of the enemy were seen coming up the trench between NIEUPORT SAP & DEVON DUMP. The party were driven off with small arm fire & bombs. It is thought the party had lost their way as they put 2 very lights up when they were close to DEVON DUMP. Harassing fire 8.900.	
	8		Between 4.30 & 5 pm enemy bombarded area H.12.c & d with 5.9s & 4.25 H.T.Ms. Freunds Shaft received a direct hit at 4.30 pm just as the gun was being laid. The dug-out & entrance were blown in. Between 10 am & 12 md enemy bombarded G.12.c 5½.0.6 with 5.9s. Between 7 pm & 8 pm flash signalling was observed from Cité St Elie. Harassing fire 4.000 rds.	
	9.		Between 2 pm & 4.30 pm enemy bombarded area in front of GEORGE'S TRENCH & also G.12.a 52.06. Harassing fire. 6.000 rds.	
	10.		St GEORGE'S TRENCH was again bombarded at intervals during the day with 5.9s 4.2s H.T.M & L.T.M. At 10.45 pm enemy put up 1 red 1 green 1 white 1 golden rain light from Trench G 12 d. No action appeared to follow. Harassing fire 5.500 rds	
	11.		Enemy projected gas shells at 1-30. in the vicinity of Stonefield Rd slight effects felt in Village Line. Harassing fire 6.000 rds	

December 1917

WAR DIARY or INTELLIGENCE SUMMARY

Page III

139th Machine Gun Company

Army Form C. 2118.

Place	Date	Hour	Summary of Events and Information	Remarks and references to Appendices
VERMELLES	12		During the raid by the 1/5th Batt S. Foresters on the enemy's 1st & 2nd B. line Trenches 29,000 rds were fired. The enemy put up a fairly heavy barrage on our front & reserve lines. At 3.50pm commenced to shell O.G.1 & O.B.1 with 5.9's & 4.2's also about 20 gas shells. Harassing fire 4.000 rds.	
	13		Between 3 & 4.15pm slight bombardment was carried out on G.12.c & d. At 10.15pm "Attack Quarqui" was received enemy bombarded ST GEORGES TRENCH. The dumps in G.12.d also received considerable attention. At 3 Am "Attack Border" was received DEVON DUMP GUN was put in action on its SOS Line & fired 1250 Rds. Harassing fire 3.500 Rds.	
	14		At 12 midday enemy shelled HULLOCH Rd. at G.16.a 9.9 with shrapnel. At 2.15pm enemy put up white very lights from trenches in G.5.c & d. Harassing fire 7.500 Rds.	
	15		Harassing fire 7.500 Rds.	
	16		Harassing fire 5.000 Rds.	
	17		During morning T.Ms have been active chiefly on the fronts of Brigades on our left.	
	18		Harassing fire 8.500 Rds.	
	19		Harassing fire 7.500 Rds.	
	20		E.A. have been active during morning A.A. Gun fired 2.500 rds Harassing fire 8000.	
	21		Slight T.M. activity between 8.Am & 10.30am. A.A. Gun fired 1000 Rds Harassing fire 9.500 Rd.	
	22		Harassing fire 6.750 Rds.	
	23		During morning enemy shelled LE RUTOIRE with H.V. & 5.9. Harassing fire 4.250 Rds.	
			Harassing fire 5000 Rd.	
	24		Between 4.30 & 10 pm enemy MGs were active on O.B.1 & Light Railway behind Harassing fire 6000 Rd.	

December 1917   Page IV

WAR DIARY
or
INTELLIGENCE SUMMARY
(Erase heading not required.)   139th Machine Gun Company

Army Form C. 2118.

Place	Date	Hour	Summary of Events and Information	Remarks and references to Appendices
VERMELLES	25		Between 6.15 & 6.45pm there was considerable activity with T.Ms on the left flank Brigade. At 7.15pm enemy put Gas Shells in G.10.B. central. At 9.pm enemy Shelled communication Trenches in G.10. & 11. with with 4.2s H.V. Harassing fire 4.500 R	
	26		At 4 pm enemy fired 3. 5.9 which fell 10 yds from position V.32 a.o.6. 1 E.A. flew low over G.12 C & d. between 10.15 & 10.45 A.M. AA Gun fired 500. Harassing fire 3.750 R	
	27		Sudley Sump had a direct hit & tripod has been damaged. Harassing fire 7000 R	
	28		Sudley Sump was again shelled with 5.9s & H.T.Ms. 6. H.V. fell on Chapel Alley near V.33.A. Harassing fire 5.200 R. AA gun fired 500 R	
	29		Harassing fire 7.750 R. AA Gun fired 1500 R	
	30		Enemy M.Gs were in action over R.E. Shaft & ST. GEORGES TRENCH during night. Harassing fire 8.250 Rds	
	31		At 1.15pm rapid hostile fire with 4.5 & 5.9s for 10 minutes all round Chapel Alley. Harassing fire 7.500 R	
			WORK DONE during month. Improved trenches at Battery. New position at R.55 Constructed. Rebuilt parados to Sudley Sump. Built new position G.17.b 67.85. Stakes put out & wired in front of R.53. Constructed Shelters for S.A.A. & kit boxes at V.32. Put in AA mounting at V.32. Alternative emplacement Constructed at R.55. Rebuilt position at Sudley Sump.	Casualties during month. 1. O.R. killed in action 2/12/17. Approx. N. of Rounds fired during month 200.550 Harassing fire 6.500 A.A. 207.050 Total. Transfer of Offrs. 2nd Lieut R PAGE Transferred to 137 MGC. Lieut D. HARVEY from 137 Coy to be OC. 4. Reinforcements during month

P.M.W. Oliver
Capt.

January 1918.

WAR DIARY or INTELLIGENCE SUMMARY.

Page I. Army Form C. 2118.

139th Machine Gun Company

Vol 24

Place	Date	Hour	REF LOOS 36.C.N.W. 1/10.000 Summary of Events and Information	Remarks and references to Appendices
VERMELLES H.Q. BREWERY	1st		At 5 am the enemy opened a heavy bombardment with T.M's & winged bombs on Tunnels & St George's Trench which was carried on for about an hour, during the raid on our left. Harassing fire 10.000 rds.	
	2nd		Harassing fire 7.500 rds. 4.0 P.M. Arr'd At 46 Div I Bat & taken on strength.	
	3rd		At 9.30 pm enemy opened heavy barrage on St George's Trench & Front Line positions At the same time S.O.S. was put up in the vicinity of Dudley Dump & 14.000 rds were fired between 9.30 & 10 p.m. Casualty No 87393 Pte Panother G.S. wound in back. Harassing fire. 6.000 rds. A.A. Gun fired 500 rds.	
	4th		Harassing fire 5.500 rds.	
	5th		Harassing fire. 5.500 rds	
	6th		Harassing fire. 4.500 rds	
	7th		Harassing fire. 9.000 rds.	
	8th		Harassing fire. 9.300 rds Lieut E.G. Holden granted leave to UK. 8.1.18 to 22.1.18	
	9th		Harassing fire. 6.000 rds	
	10th		Harassing fire. 6.500 rds.	
	11th		Harassing fire 6.000 rds. A.A. Gun fired 500 rds. Capt J.B. Baber granted leave to UK. 11.1.18 to 25.1.18. - N-108584 L/Cpl Cranmer H. arr'd 46 Div I Bn Taken on Strength No.72092 Cpl Bryan awarded Military Medal C.R.O. 9.1.18	
	12th		Between 1.30 a.m & 2. a.m. there was considerable artillery activity on the front of the 6 Division on our right. There has been also T.M. activity on the Brigade front this morning. Some E.A. over G.19.c. &d. Harassing fire 4.000 rds AA Gun 250 rds	

January 1918.   WAR DIARY or INTELLIGENCE SUMMARY.   Page II   Army Form C. 2118.

139th Machine Gun Company.

Place	Date	Hour	Summary of Events and Information	Remarks and references to Appendices
VERMELLES	13.		Slight hostile activity with 4.2s 5.9s & T.Ms during yesterday afternoon in the vicinity of G.12 c & d. Harassing fire 3.000 rds.	
	14"		The enemy shelled G.12 c & d. between 4.15 & 4.45 pm with 4.2s 5.9s & T.Ms. appeared to be trying to find our T.M emplacements. Harassing fire 5.000 rds.	
	15"		At 11.30 pm there was considerable artillery activity on the front of the Division on our right, the enemy putting up a quantity of all coloured lights, the situation became normal again at 12.15 am. This morning since 9.30 am the enemy has been shelling the T.Ms at G.12 c.50.02 with 5.9s. Harassing fire 4.500 rds.	
	16"		Between 1 & 2 pm the enemy continued the shelling of St George's Trench. Between 2.30 & 3.15 pm the enemy put a heavy barrage of H. & M.T.M. on our front & support lines in G.12 c & d. Since 11 am this morning the enemy has been shelling Philosophe. Harassing fire. 4.000 rds.	
	17"		Between 5 pm & 8 pm enemy shelled Le Rutoire with shrapnel, otherwise there is nothing to report. Harassing fire. 6.250 rds.	
	18"		Harassing fire 6.200 rds. A.A. Gun fired. 750 rds.	
	19"		At 7 pm there were 3 explosions on the front of the Brigade on our right they were thought to have been the enemy's new gas mortars, as they exploded over G.11.12.07 & 18. & 2000 rds were fired by our A.A. Guns. E.A. have been very active this morning. Harassing fire 3000	

January 1918.

WAR DIARY or INTELLIGENCE SUMMARY

Page III.

139th Machine Gun Company

Army Form C. 2118.

Place	Date	Hour	Summary of Events and Information	Remarks and references to Appendices
VERMELLES	20		This morning between 8 & 9 am. there was shelling of our reserve lines. Harassing fire 3,500 rds. Lieut W.T.B. Regis granted leave to U.K. from 20.1.18 to 3.2.18. 1 O.R. and 46 Div. I. Bar taken on Strength.	
	21st		Harassing fire 4,500 rds.	
	22nd		E.A. were active over G.12.17. & 18 during the morning. Harassing fire 3,000 rds. A.A. Gun 2,000 rds.	
	23rd		Lieut Holden ret. from Leave to UK. Company were relieved in the trenches by 34th Machine Gun Coy (11th Div). At 6 pm Coy moved to rest billets at Cense La Vallee. arrived at 9 p.m.	
CENSE LA VALLEE	24th to 27.		Programme of Training carried out in Rest Billets. Squad Drill. Physical Training. Gun Drill. Afternoon Football.	
	28 & 31.		Physical Training. Company Drill. Gun Drill. Respirator Drill. Semaphore. Indication & Recognition of Targets. Afternoon Football.	

Casualties during month.
No. 87393 Pte Carruthers G.S. Wound in back

Reinforcements during month.
6 O.R. taken on Strength of Coy.

Approx No. of Rounds fired during month.
136,750 rds.   A.A. fired 6000.

S. Harvey LT.

February 1918

WAR DIARY or INTELLIGENCE SUMMARY
Army Form C. 2118.

C Company 46 Batt M.G.C.
~~139th~~ Machine Gun Coy.

1/0. HAZEBROUCK 5A / 100,000

Place	Date	Hour	Summary of Events and Information	Remarks and references to Appendices
CENSE LA VALLEE	1st 2nd		Programme of Training while in Billet. 8 to 8.30 A.M. Physical Training under Section Sgts. Company Drill, Indication & Recognition	
	3rd to 5th		Physical Training. Section & Arms Drill. Gun Drill. Immediate Action. Afternoons. Football. Tug of War. &	
	6th to 7th		Physical Training. Mechanism. Advanced Gun Drill. Lecturing on Mechanism of the Rifle & the theory of sighting. Immediate Action.	
HURION VILLE.	8th		Company paraded at 10.15 AM & marched to HURION VILLE via BOSNETTES. BAS RIEUX. HAUT RIEUX. BURBURE. Arrived 2 p.m.	
PETIGNY.	9.		Company paraded at 9.30 AM & marched under Tactical march order (Action expected) to PETIGNY via BELLERY. AMETTES. NEDON. NEDON-CHALLE. FONTAINE-LEZ-HERMAN FEBIN-PALFART. Arrived at PETIGNY at 6 pm. Company inspected by G.O.C. whilst on march	
	10th to 15th		Physical Training. Company Drill. Combined Drill. Rifle Firing rapid loading & 5 rounds grouping practice. Indication & Recognition combined with fire orders. Rough Ground Drill. Judging distances. Pack Transport under Transport Officer	

February 1918.

WAR DIARY or INTELLIGENCE SUMMARY.

C Page II
C Company 46 Batt M.G.C.
Late 139 Machine Gun Company

Army Form C. 2118.

Place	Date	Hour	Summary of Events and Information	Remarks and references to Appendices
PETIGNY.	17th to 20th		Packing Limbers. Section Drill with limbers. Rifle firing 5 rounds grouping practice. Pack saddling. Revolver snapping practice. Physical Training. Section drill with Fighting Limbers. Barrage drill. Gas drill. Musketry practice. Machine Gun Single shot traversing practice. Barrage Drill.	
	21st to 24th		Physical Training. Musketry 5 rounds application. Machine Gun Tripod traversing practice, single loading. Section Tactical Marching order. Gas drill. Test of Elementary Training. Physical Training. Interior Economy. Barrage Drill. Rapid Loading Combined drill.	
	25th to 28th		Musketry practice. 5 rounds grouping 8" bull. 5 rounds application 2nd class figure. 20 rounds Rapid 2nd class figure. Section drill with Limbers. Barrage drill. Revolver Practice (6 rounds slow, 6 rounds rapid.) Combined drill (traversing) Musketry practice (5 rounds grouping)(5 rounds application) (15 rounds Rapid time allowed 1 minute) Barrage Scheme:- Packing Limbers. Pack mules. Barrage drill. Fire Direction. Elevating & traversing dials. Physical Training. Mechanism. Immediate Action.	
			Reinforcements. 4 O.R. during month. Evacuations 5 O.R. during month.	
			N. 24364 Sgt W. Jane awarded Croix de Guerre Auth. M.S./4/8077. of 27 & 28-1-18.	

S Harvey. Lt.
fr. O.C. 139 M.G. Coy.